From
Ordinary
To
Extraordinary

Transforming Your Dreams into
Legendary Realities

JEMIMAH CHUKS

FROM ORDINARY TO EXTRAORDINARY

Transforming Your Dreams into Legendary Realities

Copyright ©2024 by **Jemimah Chuks.**

Paperback ISBN: 978-1-965593-06-6

Hardcover ISBN: 978-1-965593-07-3

Published by Cornerstone Publishing

A Division of Cornerstone Creativity Group LLC
Info@thecornerstonepublishers.com
www.thecornerstonepublishers.com

Author's Contact

To book the author as a speaker at your next event or to order bulk copies of this book, please, use the information below:

Jemimahchuks@yahoo.com

Printed in the United States of America.

DEDICATION

This book is dedicated to the memory of my late father, **Apostle U. J. Ejikeme Uduhirinwa**. The late-night wisdom you imparted during our many conversations was, and always will be, priceless.

May your soul continue to rest in peace.

CONTENTS

CONTENTS

INTRODUCTION

Every entrepreneur's journey begins with a dream and a leap of faith. In December 2013, I took that leap, stepping off a plane onto American soil with my heart pounding with excitement and trepidation. Like many entrepreneurs embarking on a new venture, I carried dreams of success and a wealth of experience. Little did I know that this moment would begin a transformative journey that would challenge everything I thought I knew about success and resilience.

I arrived in the United States of America not as a desperate immigrant fleeing hardship but as a successful professional seeking a new horizon. I had built a thriving career as a business consultant in Nigeria, enjoying the fruits of my labor - a comfortable lifestyle, a network of influential connections in business and politics, and the warmth of a close-knit family. I left it behind for my love to join my husband and the allure of unexplored opportunities in the land of endless possibilities.

However, the America I encountered was different from my perception. The initial euphoria of my arrival quickly gave way to the harsh realities of starting anew in a foreign land. My husband, determined to provide for our new life, worked tirelessly, juggling two jobs with grueling 12-hour shifts. Our time together became a rare luxury, and our conversations were often limited to hurried exchanges as we passed each other at the door.

Despite his efforts, we struggled to make ends meet. I worked as a Certified Nursing Assistant, earning a mere $10 an hour - a far cry from the boardrooms and business deals I was used to. The dream of a better life seemed to recede each day, replaced by the grinding reality of financial struggle and cultural disorientation.

The challenges I faced were multifaceted and often overwhelming. While I spoke English, the number of accents I encountered made communication a daily hurdle. Cultural nuances and unspoken social rules created frequent misunderstandings, leaving me feeling like an outsider even in seemingly familiar situations. American systems—from healthcare to education to business—operated on principles unfamiliar to me, requiring constant adaptation and learning.

Rebuilding my professional identity from scratch proved to be the most daunting task. I had to prove myself afresh, starting from the very bottom. This process was humbling and, at times, deeply discouraging. There were moments when the weight of starting over felt insurmountable, and the temptation to give up was strong.

Yet, amidst these challenges, a spark of determination refused to be extinguished. The same drive that propelled me to success in Nigeria now fueled my resolve to overcome these new obstacles. I realized that my unique background, far from being a liability, could become my greatest asset. My diverse experiences gave me a perspective that many natives lacked. The key was finding the right avenue to channel this potential.

That avenue revealed itself in the world of real estate. However, this path was not without its own set of hurdles. The licensing exam proved to be a formidable challenge, and I failed it three times in succession. Each failure chipped away at my confidence, leaving me questioning my abilities and my place in this new world. After the third attempt, I was ready to abandon this dream, convinced that perhaps it was beyond my reach.

In this moment of doubt, a supportive voice urged me to give it one more trial. That encouragement and faith in my potential made all the difference. With renewed determination, I approached the exam for the fourth time - and passed. This experience became a cornerstone of my philosophy: setbacks are not failures but opportunities for comebacks.

Armed with my hard-won license and an unwavering drive to succeed, I threw myself into the real estate industry with every ounce of energy I possessed. I worked tirelessly, leveraging every skill I had developed throughout my diverse career. My accent, once a source of self-consciousness, became a unique identifier that clients remembered. My international background allowed me to connect with a diverse clientele, understanding their needs in ways others couldn't.

I quickly learned that success in real estate, much like in life, is not just about knowledge or skills - it's about building relationships, understanding people's dreams, and helping them manage one of the most significant decisions of their lives. My experiences gave me a unique empathy for clients going through life transitions. I could relate to their fears, hopes, and desires for a place to call home.

The results of this dedication and unique approach exceeded my wildest expectations. Within just four years, I had sold over 300 homes, generating more than $80 million in sales. I became one of the top 50 agents nationwide and made the number one position in Delaware. My journey from struggling immigrant to extraordinary success became a testament to the power of resilience, adaptability, and unwavering determination.

This rapid rise taught me valuable lessons about the nature of success in America. I realized that while the challenges for newcomers are real, so are the opportunities. The American dream is not a myth, but it requires more than hard work - it demands strategic thinking, cultural intelligence, and the ability to turn one's unique experiences into competitive advantages.

As my success grew, I began mentoring other newcomers to the industry, sharing the strategies and principles that had helped me overcome seemingly insurmountable obstacles. It was through these interactions that the idea for this book was born.

This book is a roadmap for anyone facing challenges in their personal or professional lives. Whether you're starting over in a new environment, venturing into an unfamiliar industry, or an entrepreneur battling self-doubt and fear of failure; it offers both inspiration and practical guidance. It's a beacon of hope and a strategic guide for transforming perceived disadvantages into the very fuel for your success.

Within these pages, you'll find principles I've personally tested and refined through my journey of challenges and triumphs. You'll learn how to:

- Overcome obstacles and forge your path.

- Accelerate your learning and scale your success.

- Develop unstoppable persistence.

- Capitalize on the hidden advantages of your unique background.

- Implement life-changing lessons derived from my journey.

Throughout this book, you'll find detailed accounts of how these lessons played out in my journey, from my initial struggles to my eventual success as a top real estate agent. You'll learn how I turned my accent and cultural background into unique selling points that set me apart in the industry. I'll share the techniques I used to rapidly absorb information about the American real estate market, allowing me to compete effectively with those with more years of local experience.

You'll discover the mindset shifts that enabled me to avoid repeated failures and setbacks. I'll reveal how I learned to manage the complex web of American business relationships, building a network that supported my growth and opened doors to new opportunities. You'll see how I transformed my communication style to connect more effectively with American clients while staying true to my authentic self.

But more than just my story, you'll find the tools and insights you need to write your success story. This book will guide you in identifying your passions and pursuing them with unwavering focus. You'll learn how to build resilience that can weather any storm and how to leverage your unique experiences to stand out in your chosen field. We'll delve into the importance of emotional intelligence and how to cultivate it, a critical factor in building lasting relationships and achieving long-term success.

Your journey - with all its challenges and seemingly insurmountable obstacles - is not a disadvantage. It's your superpower. The adversities you've faced, the new perspectives you've gained, and the skills you've had to develop - are all assets that set you apart in an increasingly globalized world. This book will show you how to harness these assets and turn them into your competitive advantage.

As we embark on this journey together, I want you to know that your dreams are valid, no matter how impossible they may seem now. Your ambitions are achievable, regardless of where you start from. Your potential is limitless, bounded only by your willingness to persist and grow.

Moving from the ordinary to the extraordinary means transcending the status quo, revolutionizing your field, and inspiring future generations. It is driven by a mindset shift that sees oneself as a catalyst for change and opportunities where others see obstacles.

This book is not just about surviving in a new environment or industry; it's about thriving. It's about moving beyond mere adaptation to making your mark. It's about transforming from a dreamer into a legendary success story.

Countless entrepreneurs have realized this transformation before you. This book is your companion in becoming the next extraordinary leader who inspires the next generations. No more accepting societal limits. No more letting self-doubt stifle your greatness. No more sleepless nights, wondering "What if?"

So, are you ready to begin this transformative journey? Are you prepared to challenge your limitations, rewrite your story, and step into your full potential? If your answer is yes, then turn the page. Remember, as my favorite scripture says, "I can do all things through Christ who strengthens me."[1] And so can you.

Welcome to your extraordinary future.

---

1   Philippians 4:13 (New King James Version).

Principle #1

SHARPEN YOUR FOCUS AND CLARIFY YOUR VISION

"Chase the vision, not the money; the money will end up following you."

- TONY HSIEH

Every morning in Africa, a gazelle awakens, knowing it must run faster than the fastest lion or face death. Similarly, a lion knows it must outrun the slowest gazelle or risk starving to death. Whether you are the lion or the gazelle, the principle remains: when the sun rises, you must start running.

This imagery captures the essence of focus and vision in entrepreneurship. In the wild, the lion and the gazelle are driven by an imperative: survival. The lion focuses on capturing its prey, while the gazelle focuses on evading predators. For entrepreneurs, each day presents new challenges and opportunities, reflecting the natural struggle for survival.

Success requires unwavering focus on one's vision, whether it's achieving a specific business goal, developing an innovative product, or expanding market reach. Just as the lion and the gazelle must remain vigilant and adaptable to thrive, entrepreneurs, too, must be focused and crystalize their vision in the ever-changing business landscape.

A clear vision and unwavering focus are paramount to achieving a legendary success in your field. A vision is a clear and compelling long-term goal that provides a sense of purpose and direction. It outlines what you want to accomplish and the impact you wish to create, serving as a guiding star that illuminates the path forward, especially during challenging times. Engaging actively with your vision is essential to maintain this sense of direction.

Vision is more than just an end goal; it encompasses your core values and aspirations, giving your efforts meaning and context. It is about understanding what you truly desire to achieve and why it matters. Having a clear vision motivates you to push through obstacles and stay committed even when the journey becomes difficult. This intrinsic motivation is critical for long-term success.

Focus, on the other hand, is the ability to concentrate your energy and efforts on achieving this vision. Entrepreneurs often find themselves surrounded by a sea of opportunities and distractions, which makes it easy to lose sight of their core objectives. Thus, establishing a focused vision is crucial.

This vision does not have to be grand or world-changing; it only needs to resonate with you and align with your values and aspirations.

Discovering and refining your vision requires deep self-reflection and honesty. It involves asking critical questions: What excites you? What problems do you feel compelled to solve? What impact do you want your work to have on others? Reflecting on these questions can lead to profound insights that shape your entrepreneurial journey. By understanding your motivations and aspirations, you can craft a vision that is both inspiring and attainable.

Your vision will likely evolve as you gain insights from your experiences, but it should always remain connected to your purpose. This evolving nature of vision is not a sign of instability but a reflection of growth and adaptation. As you gather more information and experience, your vision can be refined to better align with your goals and the realities of your industry. However, the essence of your vision, rooted in your values and aspirations, should remain consistent.

When I arrived in the United States in December 2013, my heart was filled with excitement and hope. I stepped off the plane, carrying dreams of success rooted in my past achievements as a business consultant in Nigeria. My aspirations were broad then, fueled by a desire to support my family and forge a prosperous life alongside my husband.

I envisioned a new chapter where my experiences would translate into opportunities, but I did not yet have a clear path defined.

As I settled into life, I was eager to explore the possibilities ahead. I wanted to build a life that not only mirrored the success I had known but exceeded it. However, I quickly realized that my vision would need to adapt to the realities of my new environment.

The first few months in America were a mix of learning and adaptation. My husband worked tirelessly to provide for us while I sought to contribute financially. I took up a job as a Certified Nursing Assistant, earning a modest income that starkly contrasted with my previous lifestyle. This role was not what I had envisioned, but I embraced it as a necessary step toward finding my footing.

When I secured the job at a doctor's office through a connection at church, I approached it with enthusiasm and a hunger to learn. The medical field was new to me, but I was determined to excel. I absorbed every bit of information I could, asking questions and observing the more experienced staff. My dedication didn't go unnoticed, and within a year, I was promoted several times, moving from an intern to a medical assistant.

However, despite my efforts and promotions, I quickly realized that the income from this job wasn't enough to support our growing needs and aspirations. This realization sparked a curiosity about career paths and opportunities in America.

DISCOVERING NEW PATHS

Driven by the need to improve our financial situation, I asked, "How can I survive here? What's the way forward?"

The responses I received were almost unanimous: "Become a nurse!" People painted an attractive picture of nurses earning $60,000-$65,000 annually, with pathways to becoming nurse practitioners or even doctors. The prospect of a stable, well-paying career in healthcare was alluring. It seemed to offer the financial security we needed and the opportunity to help others, which aligned with my values.

With hope and determination in my spirit, I enrolled in nursing programs. Little did I know that this decision would lead me to one of the most challenging periods of my life. I had never studied science before, and the academic rigor of nursing school was unlike anything I had experienced. Terms like "CH4 plus" in chemistry class might as well have been a foreign language. I found myself reading materials seven times to grasp the concepts.

The struggle was not just academic. Balancing the demands of nursing school with family responsibilities and work was exhausting. There were nights when I sat at our small kitchen table, surrounded by textbooks and notes, fighting against the urge to sleep. The weight of my aspirations clashed with the reality of my limitations, often feeling like I was drowning.

It was during this period of intense struggle that I reached a crucial turning point. Sitting in a lecture hall one day, feeling overwhelmed and out of place, I had a moment of clarity. I realized that perhaps I was forcing myself down a path that wasn't aligned with my strengths and passions.

This realization led to one of the toughest decisions I've ever made - I decided to drop out of nursing school. It wasn't an easy choice. The fear of disappointment, and being seen as a quitter, weighed heavily on me. But deep down, I knew that there had to be a better path - one that would allow me to thrive and contribute in a way that felt authentic to who I am.

This initial phase of my journey forced me to reflect on my aspirations and consider what I wanted for my future. With each day that passed, I realized that my previous dreams needed to evolve to fit the landscape I was now in. The nursing role was a means to an end, but I yearned for something to ignite my passion and utilize my skills more effectively.

During this time, I explored various career paths, each presenting its set of opportunities and challenges. I dabbled in graphic design and web development and even considered coaching, but none of these avenues felt the right fit. As I continued to explore and grow, I found myself drawn to the world of media and communication. This interest led me to an exciting new venture - "The Jemimah Show." Starting a TV show as an immigrant was a daunting prospect, but it became a crucial milestone in my journey. I felt lost initially, unsure of my path. Then, I began to understand the importance of aligning my vision with my strengths and experiences.

THE DEFINING MOMENT

Leaving nursing school taught me an invaluable lesson: don't be afraid to pivot when something isn't working. Sometimes, the path to success involves taking a step back to reassess and redirect. This realization opened my mind to possibilities I had never considered before.

One day, while driving home, I noticed a sign for a property. At the same time, I heard a realtor's voice on the radio. It felt like a sign from God urging me to pursue real estate.

Initially, I hesitated. I had already tried many different paths, and the thought of starting something new was daunting. But the idea wouldn't leave me. A few months later, I found myself looking at that same sign. I felt the Holy Spirit encouraging me to go in and express my interest in becoming a real estate agent.

Despite my doubts and fears, I decided to take a leap of faith. I walked into the office, heart pounding, and declared my intention to become a real estate agent. I attributed my visit to divine guidance, even though I lacked knowledge of the required licensing process.

The realtor I spoke to was patient and kind. She gave me the information I needed to enroll in a real estate school and encouraged me to pursue this path. Her support and guidance were crucial in those early days, giving me the confidence to take my first steps into real estate.

Once I had this vision - to become a successful real estate entrepreneur and help others achieve their dreams of homeownership; everything changed. My focus sharpened. Every decision I made, including the skills I sought to develop was in the service of this vision.

As I learned more about it, I began to see a connection between my past experiences and the potential within this field. Real estate offered a unique platform where I could leverage my background in business consulting, understand client needs, and facilitate significant life transitions for others. It felt like a natural progression - a way to not only reshape my professional identity but also to create meaningful connections with clients. I realized that real estate was not just a job; it was an opportunity to channel my experiences and empathy into helping others find their homes.

With my vision taking shape - becoming a trusted real estate professional who understood the diverse needs of clients and could understand the complexities of the market, I was ready to commit wholeheartedly to the real estate industry. I enrolled in a licensing course, embracing the challenge of mastering the material that would qualify me for this new path.

I was driven by a newfound clarity of purpose, even when the journey ahead would not be easy. My evolving vision was no longer a vague aspiration but a specific goal that aligned with my unique strengths and experiences.

I ALMOST GAVE UP

As I stepped into the world of real estate, I carried with me the lessons learned from my past. I understood that success would not happen overnight but requires focus and perseverance - I was ready to leap. The challenges I had faced became stepping stones, fueling my determination to achieve my vision of becoming a successful real estate professional.

I committed myself to the process, immersing myself in the coursework required for the licensing exam. Each study session felt like a step closer to achieving my license and solidifying my identity as a real estate professional.

I attended networking events, connecting with established agents and absorbing their insights about the industry. These interactions expanded my understanding of the market and helped me cultivate relationships that would prove invaluable as I built my brand. I began to see how my unique background could resonate with clients and set me apart from others in the field.

Despite my enthusiasm, I faced a significant setback early on - I failed the qualifying exam. For someone who had always prided herself on academic achievement, failure was devastating. It shook my confidence and made me question whether I was cut out for this field.

But I refused to give up. I saw this failure not as an end but as a challenge to overcome. I doubled down on my studies, spending every free moment poring over textbooks and practice exams. I retook the exam, only to fail again.

The process was grueling and impersonal. Unlike other systems I was familiar with, there was no room for discussion or appeal - the computer's decision was final. After my third unsuccessful attempt, I faced a crossroads. The rules dictated that I would need to retake the entire course before attempting the exam again.

This series of failures led to a crisis of faith. I began to doubt myself and my decision to pursue real estate. I thought, "Maybe I didn't hear God correctly. Maybe real estate isn't the right business for me." The dream I had built up in my mind - of becoming a successful realtor, having my real estate page, of achieving my goals - seemed to crumble around me.

In despair, I threw my real estate books in the trash. It felt like admitting defeat, like closing the door on this chapter of my life. The pivotal moment came when a supportive voice urged me to give it another trial, reminding me that resilience is often the bridge to success.

With renewed focus and confidence, I approached the exam for the fourth time.

HARNESSING CONFIDENCE FOR A CLEAR VISION

Through my experiences, I learned that self-reflection is crucial; taking the time to discover what truly excites you helps clarify your aspirations. Self-reflection involves understanding your passions, strengths, and values, which serve as the foundation for your vision. I realized that a vision is not set in stone; it evolves as you gain new insights and experiences. This evolving nature of vision is a testament to your growth and adaptability. Staying focused amid distractions requires discipline and intentionality, allowing you to remain aligned with your goals. Discipline in maintaining your focus involves setting clear priorities and developing habits that support your long-term objectives.

The journey to achieving egendary success is often paved with challenges that test our resolve. Each setback is not a final defeat but an opportunity to recalibrate our vision and sharpen our focus. These obstacles serve as learning experiences, pushing us to develop new strategies and refine our goals. They catalyze growth, prompting us to reassess our direction and determine the best way forward. Embracing them with a positive mindset transforms them into stepping stones toward success.

The Journey of the Tortoise and the Elephant as recounted in Igbo traditional stories highlights the importance of this principle. Tortoise and the elephant once set out on a long and arduous journey together. The elephant, with its immense size and strength, was confident that it would easily outpace the tortoise. It surged ahead with assurance, believing that its advantage in speed and power would ensure a swift victory. In contrast, the tortoise moved at a slow and steady pace, its focus unwavering and its eyes fixed on the distant goal.

As the journey progressed, the elephant's initial lead became a source of overconfidence. The grandeur of its speed led it to grow complacent. It began to tire and was easily distracted by the surroundings, losing sight of the primary objective. The elephant's confidence in its early advantage gradually turned into a weakness, as fatigue and distractions slowed its progress.

Meanwhile, the tortoise, despite its slower pace, maintained a consistent and deliberate approach. It did not waver from its path or allow itself to be sidetracked. The tortoise's unyielding focus on the destination enabled it to persevere through the challenges and obstacles it faced. In the end, the tortoise's steady determination paid off. It caught up with the weary elephant and surpassed it, reaching the destination first.

Just as the tortoise, with its unyielding focus, achieves its goals despite the formidable elephant's presence, entrepreneurs who maintain a clear vision and consistent focus will overcome challenges and achieve success.

Focusing on your vision helps you make informed decisions and manage distractions effectively. In the dynamic world of entrepreneurship, distractions are inevitable. New opportunities, emerging trends, and unexpected challenges can easily divert your attention. However, a strong focus on your vision enables you to evaluate these distractions critically. You can determine whether they align with your long-term goals or if they are mere diversions. This discernment is crucial in maintaining your trajectory toward a legendary success.

Moreover, focus requires discipline. It involves setting clear priorities and managing your time and resources effectively. Developing routines and habits that support your vision can help maintain this focus. Regularly revisiting your vision and assessing your progress ensures that you stay on track and make necessary adjustments along the way.

Engaging with your vision also means communicating it effectively to your team and stakeholders. A shared vision fosters a sense of unity and purpose within your organization. When everyone understands and believes in the vision, they are more likely to contribute positively and work collaboratively toward achieving it. This collective effort amplifies your potential for success.

By defining what you want to achieve and concentrating your efforts on this goal, you create a roadmap for your entrepreneurial journey. This combination of vision and focus not only guides you through challenges but also inspires and motivates you to reach new heights. As you travel your path, remember that your vision is your compass, and your focus is the drive that keeps you moving forward.

HOW TO APPLY THE PRINCIPLES OF FOCUS AND VISION

1. Engage in Self-Reflection

Engaging in self-reflection is crucial for uncovering your true passions and strengths. Set aside weekly time to ponder your interests, values, and experiences. Ask yourself questions like, "What activities make me lose track of time?" and "What issues do I feel compelled to address?" Journaling can be an effective tool, allowing you to capture your thoughts and feelings. You may also find it beneficial to seek feedback from trusted friends or mentors, as they can provide insights into your strengths that you might overlook.

Self-reflection is not a one-time event; it's an ongoing process. As you grow and change, revisiting your self-reflection can help you stay aligned with your evolving vision and ensure your entrepreneurial journey remains fulfilling and true to your authentic self. Consider setting a reminder on your calendar to revisit these reflections periodically to help you stay grounded in your goals and aspirations.

2. Define Your Vision

Once you've engaged in self-reflection, it's time to articulate your vision clearly. Write down your vision statement and ensure it captures your aspirations and the impact you wish to make. Keep it concise and specific to make it easier to remember. Share your vision with peers, mentors, or accountability partners; their feedback can refine your statement further. Additionally, consider creating a vision board that visually represents your goals to allow you to see your aspirations daily. Revisiting your vision regularly is vital, as it can evolve with your experiences and insights. Set reminders to reflect on your vision, ensuring that it remains at the forefront of your entrepreneurial journey and continues to inspire and motivate you as you navigate challenges and opportunities.

3. Set Clear Goals

Breaking your vision into clear, actionable goals is essential for tracking progress and maintaining motivation. Start by identifying the milestones that will lead you toward your larger vision. These smaller, manageable goals provide a sense of achievement and make the overall journey less overwhelming. Use the SMART criteria (Specific, Measurable, Achievable, Relevant, Time-bound) to formulate your goals.

For example, if your vision is to launch a business, your immediate goal might be to conduct market research within a specific timeframe. Regularly review and adjust your goals based on your progress and experiences. Celebrate small victories along the way, as acknowledging these achievements can boost your confidence and motivation. Remember that setting clear goals creates a roadmap for your journey, allowing you to maintain focus on your vision and adapt as needed while building momentum toward your ultimate success.

4. Cultivate a Supportive Network

Surround yourself with like-minded individuals to foster an environment of encouragement, motivation, and shared learning. Seek mentors, industry professionals, and fellow entrepreneurs who can offer guidance and insights based on their experiences. Attend networking events, workshops, and industry conferences to expand your connections and engage with those who inspire you.

Online platforms like LinkedIn or local entrepreneurial groups can also facilitate networking and foster community. Make a habit of sharing your vision and goals with your network to hold yourself accountable, and spark collaborations, and opportunities you may not have anticipated. Remember that relationships are a two-way street, so be prepared to offer support and encouragement to others. A support system can make all the difference when facing challenges and pursuing your vision.

5. View Setbacks Positively

Challenges and setbacks are inevitable parts of the entrepreneurial journey, but your mindset toward them can significantly impact your success. Instead of viewing setbacks as failures, reframe them as valuable learning experiences. Each challenge presents an opportunity to assess your approach, identify areas for improvement, and strengthen your resilience.

When facing a setback, take a moment to reflect on what went wrong and what lessons were learned. This reflective practice can foster adaptability and innovation, helping you to refine your strategies moving forward. Maintain a positive outlook by focusing on your long-term vision and reminding yourself of the progress you've made. By embracing setbacks as catalysts for growth, you build resilience and cultivate a mindset that thrives on overcoming obstacles in pursuit of your vision.

Having a clear vision and unwavering focus is foundational for any entrepreneur. Embrace the journey of discovery as you refine your vision, and remember that the path to success is rarely linear. By maintaining your commitment to your vision, you'll be more equipped to manage the inevitable challenges and setbacks that arise. Let your vision inspire and motivate you to reach new heights, creating a lasting impact in your field.

REFLECT AND ACT

1. What is your current entrepreneurial vision, and how does it align with your values and aspirations?

2. Identify three potential distractions in your current work environment that may be hindering your focus. How can you minimize their impact?

3. Who in your network can serve as an accountability partner to help you stay committed to your vision and goals?

4. How can you better articulate your vision to inspire and motivate your team?

5. What strategies can you implement to ensure your vision evolves with the changing market dynamics?

6. How do you plan to measure the progress of your vision over the next year?

7. What specific actions will you take this month to bring your vision closer to reality?

Principle #2

DEVELOP UNSHAKEABLE SELF-BELIEF WITH DETERMINATION

"Believe in yourself and all that you are. Know that there is something inside you that is greater than any obstacle."

– CHRISTIAN D. LARSON

Self-belief and determination are crucial components of entrepreneurial success. These intertwined qualities form the bedrock upon which visionaries build their empires, transforming ideas into tangible realities. At its core, self-belief is an unwavering confidence in one's abilities, coupled with the conviction that goals are attainable despite inevitable obstacles.

The baobab tree; often referred to as the "Tree of Life," stands as a symbol of self-belief and determination. With its towering presence and deep roots that anchor it firmly in the earth, the baobab is a living testament to resilience.

Despite enduring some of the harshest conditions in nature - scorching heat, drought, and nutrient-poor soil - it not only survives but thrives, providing nourishment and shelter to the ecosystems around it.

This tree's ability to flourish against the odds mirrors the journey of entrepreneurs who must cultivate unwavering self-belief to navigate the challenges of their path. Just as the baobab's roots dig deep to find sustenance, entrepreneurs must dig deep within themselves to find the determination needed to push forward, even when faced with adversity. The baobab's longevity and strength are not accidental; they are the result of years of persistent growth and adaptation. Similarly, an entrepreneur's success is built on the foundation of an enduring belief in their vision and the relentless pursuit of their goals.

In a world where obstacles are inevitable, the baobab reminds us that self-belief and determination are essential. These qualities enable us to stand tall and thrive, no matter the circumstances. Just as the baobab sustains life around it, an entrepreneur's determination fuels their ability to overcome challenges and achieve lasting success.

This mindset catalyzes bold action. Entrepreneurs with strong self-belief are more inclined to seize opportunities, even when they involve significant risks. They view challenges not as insurmountable barriers, but as chances to innovate and grow. This perspective allows them to navigate the uncertain terrain of business with greater ease and adaptability.

Determination, the steadfast resolve to pursue objectives, naturally flows from self-belief. It manifests as persistence in the face of setbacks and resilience when confronted with failure. Determined entrepreneurs don't simply give up when they encounter difficulties; instead, they analyze, learn, and adjust their strategies accordingly.

The entrepreneurial journey is often fraught with unpredictability. Market conditions fluctuate, consumer preferences shift, and unforeseen obstacles emerge. In these moments, self-belief acts as an internal compass, guiding entrepreneurs through turbulent waters. It provides the courage to make difficult decisions and the strength to stand by them, even when doubts creep in.

As Henry Ford famously said, "Whether you think you can, or you think you can't - you're right."[2] This quote encapsulates the profound impact of self-belief on entrepreneurial success. It underscores the power of mindset in shaping outcomes, suggesting that an entrepreneur's belief in their ability to succeed can become a self-fulfilling prophecy. This principle applies not only to individual challenges but to the overall trajectory of an entrepreneurial venture.

As I embarked on my journey into the real estate industry, I quickly realized that having self-belief was as crucial as defining my vision. Each day brought new challenges, and

---

2   "Whether you think you can, or you think you can't - you're right."
Commonly attributed to Henry Ford

there were moments when doubt crept in. It was easy to feel overwhelmed, especially during the rigorous preparations for the licensing exam and the uncertainty of breaking into a competitive field.

After failing the licensing exam three times, I was at a crossroads. Each failure felt like a significant setback, and my confidence began to waver. While I questioned my decision to pursue a career in real estate and wondered if I was truly capable of succeeding in such a demanding industry, I understood that my journey was not defined by these setbacks but by my ability to rise from them.

When my husband came home and saw the books in the trash, he was shocked. "Why are your books in the trash?" he asked. I told him, "It's established. Real estate isn't for me. I'm not going back to school again."

But my husband, my supporter, and vision partner, refused to let me give up. He insisted, "You will go back. You can't give up." His belief in my potential, even when my faith faltered, was a turning point. He saw in me what I couldn't see in myself at that moment - the potential to succeed, the strength to overcome this obstacle.

With my husband's encouragement, I agreed to try again. He registered me for the real estate course once more, demonstrating his unwavering support for my dreams. This act of faith and love became a cornerstone of my eventual success.

As if the challenge of passing the exam wasn't enough, I soon discovered I was pregnant. This news added another layer of complexity to an already difficult situation. I thought, "I didn't pass when I wasn't pregnant. How will I pass now?"

But instead of letting this news discourage me, I chose to see it as added motivation. I was no longer just studying for myself but for the future of my child. This perspective shift gave me renewed energy and determination. I realized that the key to overcoming my challenges lay in my self-belief - my mindset shifted from one of doubt to one of confidence.

My husband's support during this time was invaluable. He dropped me off at class every day and waited for me through the longest sessions. At night, when fatigue threatened to overwhelm me, he would wake me up to study, quizzing me while I struggled to stay awake with my growing belly. He brought me water and napkins to keep me alert and focused.

After completing the new class and months of rigorous preparation, the day of the exam arrived once again. The exam lasted four hours, each minute feeling like an eternity. When it was over, the exam supervisor insisted I take my result paper. My hands shook as I received it, and I couldn't bring myself to read it.

I sat in the car, overwhelmed with emotion, and called my husband. "How did it go?" he asked. "I don't know. I can't look at it," I replied, my voice trembling. He urged me to open it, saying, "If you didn't pass, you'll try again. But I know you passed because you studied." We went back and forth for an hour, his calm assurance battling against my fear of disappointment.

Finally, gathering all my courage, I opened the paper. The moment I saw the result, a wave of relief and joy washed over me. I had passed. All the late nights, the sacrifices, the tears, and the unwavering support of my husband had paid off. I was now officially a licensed real estate agent.

Self-belief has a profound impact on an entrepreneur's ability to inspire and lead others. Team members, investors, and customers are more likely to rally behind a leader who exudes confidence and determination. This creates a positive feedback loop, where the entrepreneur's self-belief bolsters the faith of those around them, further reinforcing their convictions.

However, it's important to note that self-belief should be grounded in reality. Successful entrepreneurs balance confidence with humility, recognizing their strengths while acknowledging areas for improvement. They seek feedback, continuously learn, and refine their approaches based on real-world experiences.

Ultimately, self-belief and determination are powerful tools that enable entrepreneurs to transform their visions into reality. They provide the courage to take calculated risks, the resilience to weather storms, and the perseverance to see projects through to completion. In the dynamic world of entrepreneurship, these qualities often mark the difference between those who merely dream and those who achieve.

As an African proverb wisely states, "The lion does not turn around when a small dog barks." True self-belief allows individuals to remain focused on their goals, undeterred by minor distractions or criticisms. This kind of self-belief was exemplified by Nelson Mandela. Despite spending 27 years in prison under harsh conditions, Mandela never wavered in his belief that South Africa could overcome apartheid. His self-belief and determination not only sustained him through those years but also enabled him to lead his nation to freedom and reconciliation. Mandela's journey is a reminder that unwavering self-belief, even in the face of seemingly insurmountable challenges, can lead to extraordinary achievements.

RESILIENCE AS A FOUNDATION FOR SELF-BELIEF

My experience taught me that success isn't about avoiding failures but persevering through them. After failing the licensing exam three times, each setback tested my resolve. I realized that self-belief can waver, even when pursuing our most cherished goals. The key lesson was that momentary doubt doesn't have to define our path. My initial decision to quit, followed by my determination to try again, showed me that self-belief is a choice we must continually make.

I discovered the crucial role that support from loved ones plays in maintaining self-belief. My husband's unwavering faith in my abilities served as a mirror, reflecting the potential I couldn't see in myself at that moment. This support was a lifeline during my lowest points, reminding me I was not alone in my struggles. This experience taught me the importance of surrounding ourselves with people who believe in us, especially when our beliefs falter.

I also recognized that self-belief and determination require tangible action. The practical support I received - being driven to class, quizzed, and encouraged to stay focused - demonstrated that believing in oneself isn't just a mental exercise; it's about creating an environment and habits that support our goals. I learned that taking consistent and small steps can lead to significant progress.

Ultimately, my success in passing the exam after multiple attempts proved that self-belief and determination are not about avoiding failure but about persisting despite it. This journey showed me how important resilience is - highlighting that how we respond to setbacks determines our overall success. It is a testament to the power of resilience and the importance of viewing setbacks as temporary obstacles rather than permanent defeats.

The key to resilience lies in acknowledging that setbacks are part of the journey. Each failure became a stepping stone, a chance to learn and adapt. This perspective shift transformed my approach to challenges, viewing them not as barriers but as opportunities for growth. With each attempt, my understanding deepened, and my strategies improved, reinforcing my self-belief.

Support from my husband wasn't just emotional; it was also practical. He took on extra responsibilities, giving me the time and space to study. This tangible support system was crucial in maintaining my focus and determination. It showed me that resilience is bolstered by a strong support network that offers both encouragement and practical help.

Additionally, I learned to create an environment conducive to success. This meant setting up a dedicated study space, establishing a consistent routine, and seeking out resources that would aid my preparation. These actions were instrumental in building a disciplined approach to overcoming obstacles.

Resilience also taught me the value of self-compassion. Understanding that it's okay to fail and that each failure is a learning experience helped me to stay motivated and reduce self-doubt. This mindset shift was essential in maintaining my confidence throughout the process.

Through these experiences, I came to understand that resilience is not just about bouncing back but about moving forward with greater wisdom and strength. It is this forward momentum, driven by resilience and supported by self-belief, that ultimately leads to success. Each step, no matter how small, contributed to a foundation of self-belief that was unshakeable, even in the face of repeated setbacks.

My journey reinforced that resilience is the cornerstone of self-belief. It's the ability to persist through challenges, supported by loved ones, and fortified by a conducive environment and practical actions. This resilience shapes our path to success, proving that setbacks are merely setups for comebacks. With each obstacle overcome, our self-belief grows stronger, guiding us toward our goals with renewed determination and confidence.

HOW TO STRENGTHEN YOUR SELF-BELIEF

1. Acknowledge Your Strengths and Achievements

Start each day by recognizing your progress, no matter how small. Consider setting aside time each morning for this reflection, allowing yourself to feel gratitude for your accomplishments. Keep a journal where you jot down three things you've accomplished or learned daily. Whether you've made a breakthrough in market research, successfully pitched your business idea to potential investors, or simply stayed consistent in your efforts, celebrate these achievements as stepping stones to greater success. Over time, reviewing these entries can provide you with motivation and insight into your growth. Reflecting on your strengths and accomplishments boosts your confidence and motivates you to keep pushing forward.

2. Practice Positive Self-Talk

Our inner dialogue shapes our reality. When negative thoughts arise, acknowledge them, but don't let them dominate your mindset. It's essential to recognize that everyone experiences self-doubt; you're not alone in this journey. Reframe negative thoughts into positive affirmations. For example, replace "I'm not cut out for this industry" with "I bring unique perspectives and skills that set me apart in this industry." Creating a list of affirmations you can refer to daily can be a powerful tool. Regularly practicing positive self-talk helps build a resilient mindset, enabling you to face challenges with confidence and optimism.

3. Seek Support and Mentorship

Surround yourself with a supportive network of fellow entrepreneurs and mentors who can provide guidance, encouragement, and valuable insights. Consider joining online forums or local groups that align with your business interests. Engage with entrepreneurial communities, attend networking events, and seek out mentorship programs tailored to your industry and business goals. A strong support system provides new perspectives, shares experiences, and helps you approach the entrepreneurial journey with increased confidence. Remember, your network can be a significant resource for accountability and motivation, pushing you to achieve your best.

4. Understand Your 'Why'

Reflect deeply on your reasons for pursuing entrepreneurship. What inspired you to embark on this journey? Consider writing a personal mission statement to clarify your intentions and aspirations. Understanding your purpose and motivations strengthens your resolve and provides clarity during challenging times. Mark Twain once said, "The two most important days in your life are the day you are born and the day you find out why."[3] This emphasizes the importance of discovering your purpose. Write down your motivations and keep them visible, perhaps on a vision board with images and quotes to stay inspired. Reviewing this vision regularly can serve as a powerful reminder of your commitment.

5. Learn from Setbacks

When setbacks occur, analyze the situation objectively to understand what went wrong. Take a step back and approach this analysis with curiosity rather than judgment. Identify valuable lessons learned and apply them to refine your approach. Seek inspiration from success stories of entrepreneurs who have faced and overcome similar challenges. Study their strategies, adapt them to fit your unique vision, and implement the necessary changes. This process can help demystify failure, showing it as an integral part of the journey rather than a stopping point. This proactive approach not only enables you

---

3   "The two most important days in your life are the day you are born and the day you find out why." commonly attributed to Twain, Mark.

to grow but also builds resilience, making you better prepared for future obstacles and more determined to achieve your goals.

Every successful entrepreneur has faced moments of doubt and uncertainty. What sets them apart is their unwavering self-belief and determination to pursue their dreams. You possess the same potential within you. Embrace your entrepreneurial journey with confidence, knowing that your current status doesn't define you; your creativity and determination do.

Self-belief is a critical ingredient in the recipe for entrepreneurial success. By nurturing your confidence and determination, you position yourself to overcome challenges and pursue your vision with unwavering commitment. Self-belief is not merely a feeling; it is an active choice cultivated through intentional practices. Trust in your abilities, view setbacks as opportunities for growth and remain steadfast in your pursuit of success.

REFLECT AND ACT

1. What are three of your greatest strengths as an entrepreneur, and how can you leverage them more effectively in your business?

2. Can you recall a recent challenge you overcame? How did this experience reinforce your self-belief?

3. What negative self-talk patterns do you notice in yourself, and how can you reframe them into positive affirmations?

4. How can you build on your past successes to boost your confidence in future endeavors?

5. What steps can you take to develop a more resilient mindset in the face of setbacks?

6. How do you plan to cultivate a supportive environment that encourages self-belief among your team?

7. What new skills or knowledge areas can you pursue to strengthen your confidence as a leader?

Principle #3

PERSEVERE WITH THE STRENGTH OF ENDURANCE

"It always seems impossible until it's done."

- NELSON MANDELA

Endurance is a cornerstone of entrepreneurial success. It involves the capacity to withstand prolonged hardships and persist through challenges with resilience and determination. Unlike short bursts of effort, sustained commitment requires sustained commitment over time, enabling you to overcome obstacles and achieve long-term goals. This quality means not giving up when faced with setbacks, but rather, pushing forward despite failures, disappointments, and the inevitable difficulties that come with pursuing ambitious goals. Entrepreneurs who cultivate endurance develop a mindset that sees challenges as opportunities for growth, turning each hurdle into a stepping stone rather than a roadblock.

The entrepreneurial path demands an indomitable spirit that withstands trials and setbacks. It requires individuals whose dreams shine brighter than the obstacles they face. Endurance is your guiding star on this journey, embodying patience to weather delays, resilience to bounce back from setbacks, and persistence to keep moving forward. It will be the compass, shield, and fuel that propel you through challenges toward your entrepreneurial vision.

Leo Tolstoy wisely said, "The two most powerful warriors are patience and time."[4] Patience allows us to weather initial storms, financial challenges, and professional setbacks. It gives us the resilience to continue learning, growing, and improving even when immediate results aren't visible. Imagine your entrepreneurial journey as planting a tree. You can't expect a mighty oak to appear overnight. It takes time, nurturing, and weathering many storms before that seed grows into something magnificent. Patience is understanding that true, lasting success is rarely an overnight phenomenon. It's about recognizing that progress, while sometimes frustratingly slow, is still progress.

Time, the other warrior Tolstoy mentions, is equally crucial. It allows for the compound effect of our efforts to take hold, providing opportunities for learning, building networks, and gaining the experience and insights that can set us apart in our

---

4   "The two most powerful warriors are patience and time." commonly attributed to Leo Tolstoy

industries. Both patience and time create a powerful force that can propel an entrepreneur from startup founder to industry icon.

After overcoming initial challenges and passing the real estate licensing exam, my journey into the real estate industry was far from smooth. I obtained my license in February 2020, and the baby arrived the same week. While nursing the baby, a pandemic hit, and then there was a shutdown. I couldn't do business, and it was a lot on my husband. I couldn't work either, but then in May, in the middle of the pandemic, I got up - the hunger was too much. I started showing houses in the middle of the pandemic and caught COVID-19 five times.

This was a period of intense trials. The pandemic created widespread fear, yet despite these challenges, I remained persistent and sold my first home just six months after obtaining my license. People cautioned me that it was the wrong time to enter the market, but endurance means pushing forward even when the odds are stacked against you. It means finding the inner strength to keep going, even when external circumstances are daunting.

I remember those early days when it felt like I was taking one step forward and two steps back. There were nights when doubt crept in, whispering that I had made a mistake in starting this venture. But then, something remarkable would happen. Inspiration struck at unexpected moments, guiding me to resources that helped my marketing efforts. I took courses, watched videos, and trusted the process, which ultimately brought everything together.

The days leading up to my first closing were particularly challenging. Despite my hard-earned license, finding clients and closing deals felt like an uphill battle. I faced numerous rejections, and each one took a toll on my confidence. The competition was fierce, and the market was tough. Days came when I questioned my decision to pursue real estate, wondering if I had what it took to succeed.

However, I reminded myself of the journey that had brought me to this point. The countless hours of studying, my determination to pass the exam despite setbacks, and the unwavering support of my husband all fueled my commitment to succeed. This realization reignited my endurance and pushed me to keep going even when times were tough.

One experience stands out vividly. After weeks of working with a potential client, showing several properties, and investing significant time and effort, I was crushed when the client chose to work with another agent. It felt like all my hard work had been in vain.

At that moment, I had two choices: allow this setback to define me or use it as motivation to improve and persevere. I chose the latter. I analyzed what went wrong, sought feedback from colleagues, and identified areas for improvement. I learned that enduring disappointments and learning from them was crucial for my growth.

I began approaching each day with renewed determination. I set specific goals, refined my strategies, and continuously sought ways to enhance my skills. I attended workshops, networked with experienced agents, and immersed myself in learning everything I could about the real estate market. My focus shifted from immediate success to building a sustainable and thriving career.

Gradually, my efforts paid off. Six months after obtaining my license, I closed my first house - a milestone that marked the beginning of my success in the industry. This achievement reinforced my belief in the power of endurance. The challenges did not disappear, but my ability to manage them improved.

According to an Ethiopian proverb, "He who learns, teaches." This reflects how my journey of endurance wasn't just about personal success; it became a lesson I could share with others, proving that through persistence and determination, the most challenging circumstances can be overcome.

EMBRACING ENDURANCE FOR LASTING SUCCESS

Endurance has become a guiding principle that informs my actions and decisions, serving as a reminder that every step, no matter how small, contributes to my overall success. I learned that perseverance is crucial, especially during unprecedented challenges like the pandemic. Despite the fear and uncertainty surrounding me, I found the strength to rise each day and start showing houses, driven by a relentless determination to succeed. This determination wasn't just about pushing through; it involved embracing the unknown and finding opportunities within it. Embracing uncertainty became essential, allowing me to adapt quickly to changing circumstances. In many ways, it was this adaptability that became my greatest ally, helping me stay agile in a landscape that was continually shifting.

Motivation in difficult times proved vital; I drew on my inner drive to push forward, even after contracting COVID-19 multiple times. These experiences tested my physical and mental limits, but they also brightened my capacity for resilience. I realized that it was during these challenging moments that my true character was revealed. Setbacks, such as losing a potential client to another agent, became valuable learning opportunities. I analyzed what went wrong, sought feedback, and refined my approach, understanding that endurance means viewing challenges as stepping stones rather than roadblocks. Each setback was an invitation to learn, to recalibrate my strategies, and to come back with renewed vigor. This perspective allowed me to reframe my experiences and approach each day with a fresh mindset.

Continuous learning and growth played a key role in my journey. I enrolled in courses, attended workshops, and networked with experienced agents to enhance my skills. This commitment to growth helped me stay relevant in an ever-changing market, equipping me with the tools needed to face new challenges. Engaging with other professionals allowed me to gain insights into best practices and emerging trends, which further fueled my passion for the industry. Celebrating small wins, like selling my first home amidst the pandemic, reinforced the power of persistence and highlighted the cumulative impact of small achievements. Each victory, no matter how minor, served as a reminder that progress is made incrementally, encouraging me to stay the course even when the path seemed daunting.

Ultimately, embracing endurance taught me that true success is not achieved overnight but through sustained effort and resilience. It is about building a foundation of perseverance that can withstand the trials of the journey. This mindset helped me stay committed to my vision through the ups and downs of my journey. If patience is about the journey, resilience is about how you handle the bumps along the way. Resilience is your ability to bounce back from setbacks, to stand up one more time than you've been knocked down. It's a testament to the strength of the human spirit, demonstrating that we are capable of overcoming challenges that once seemed insurmountable. In this journey, failure is not just a possibility - it's almost inevitable.

As Tom Hopkins is often credited with saying, "I am not judged by the number of times I fail, but by the number of times I succeed. And the number of times I succeed is in direct proportion to the number of times I can fail and keep on trying,"[5] Each failure is an opportunity to learn, adapt, and return stronger. This perspective allows us to view failure not as a dead end but as a crucial part of the learning process, propelling us toward our goals.

When Howard Schultz, the former CEO of Starbucks joined Starbucks in 1982, the company was a small coffee bean retailer in Seattle. Inspired by a trip to Italy, where he experienced the vibrant coffee culture, Schultz envisioned transforming Starbucks into a chain of coffeehouses that served not only coffee but also provided a welcoming community space.

Initially, Schultz's vision faced resistance from the company's founders, who were hesitant to change the business model. Undeterred, he left to establish his coffee chain, Il Giornale, to prove that his vision could succeed. After demonstrating the concept's viability, Schultz acquired Starbucks in 1987 and began expanding it.

However, the journey was fraught with challenges. Financial difficulties and market skepticism threatened the company's growth. Despite these setbacks, Schultz's endurance "built Starbucks from a local business with 6 stores and less than 100 employees into a

---

5 "I am not judged by the number of times I fail, but by the number of times I succeed. And the number of times I succeed is in direct proportion to the number of times I can fail and keep on trying," commonly attributed to Tom Hopkins.

national one with more than 1,300 stores and 25,000 employees."[6] His unwavering commitment to his long-term vision and ability to persevere through obstacles underscore the critical role endurance plays in achieving sustained success.

Endurance is not just about physical stamina but also about mental and emotional strength. It requires a positive attitude, a resilient spirit, and the ability to maintain focus and motivation over the long haul. By cultivating endurance, entrepreneurs can manage the ups and downs of their journey, stay committed to their vision, and ultimately achieve success.

By embracing endurance, I developed the mental and emotional strength needed to overcome obstacles and achieve my long-term goals, reminding me that with resilience and determination, any obstacle can be surmounted. This journey of endurance has taught me that true strength lies in our ability to persist, adapt, and ultimately thrive in the face of adversity. Each challenge we encounter contributes to our growth, shaping us into the individuals we aspire to become. As we build our endurance, we not only enhance our capacity for success but also deepen our understanding of our potential. This journey is not just about reaching the destination; it's about becoming the person we need to be along the way.

Moreover, I learned that endurance is not solely about

---

6   Howard Schultz, *Pour Your Heart Into It: How Starbucks Built a Company One Cup at a Time* (New York: Hyperion, 1997), 10.

individual effort; it often requires a community of support. Throughout my career, I sought out mentors and peers who provided encouragement and guidance. These connections reminded me that I am not alone in my struggles. When the weight of challenges felt overwhelming, it was the solidarity and encouragement from my network that often reignited my passion. They provided fresh perspectives, helping me see the light at the end of the tunnel even when it felt distant. As I reflect on my journey, I recognize that building a strong support system is crucial for sustaining endurance over the long haul.

Additionally, I discovered the importance of self-care in maintaining endurance. As I faced the rigors of my career, I realized that neglecting my well-being would eventually lead to burnout. Implementing regular self-care routines, such as exercise, meditation, and time for hobbies, became essential to preserving my energy and enthusiasm. Taking time for myself not only rejuvenated my spirit but also provided clarity in decision-making, enhancing my overall performance. This balance between work and self-care proved vital for long-term success, reminding me that I must prioritize my health to achieve my goals effectively.

Embracing endurance has been transformative, teaching me that success is a marathon, not a sprint. By cultivating resilience, seeking support, and practicing self-care, I've equipped myself with the tools to handle the complexities of my journey. Every challenge faced and every setback encountered has added layers to my understanding, preparing me to take on future endeavors with confidence and grit. With endurance as my foundation, I approach each day with renewed optimism, knowing that the journey ahead is filled with possibilities waiting to be seized. In this pursuit of success, I embrace endurance as my steadfast companion, guiding me through both triumphs and tribulations alike.

HOW TO BUILD ENDURANCE

1. Understand that progress may be slow but steady

Keep track of your achievements, no matter how small. Each new client acquired, each problem solved, and each skill improved are all steps forward. Consider maintaining a progress journal where you document these small victories daily. At the end of each week, review your entries. You'll likely be surprised by how much you've accomplished. This practice not only helps you recognize your progress but also reinforces the idea that steady, consistent effort leads to significant growth over time. Remember, even on days when you feel like your business is standing still, you're still gaining valuable experience and insight that will serve you well in the future.

2. Avoid the trap of comparing your journey to others

Every business's path is unique. The startup that seems to have overnight success might be facing challenges you can't see. Focus on your progress. It's easy to fall into the comparison trap, especially in the age of social media, where everyone's highlight reel is on display. But remember, you're seeing their curated successes, not their daily struggles. If you find yourself feeling discouraged by others' apparent success, take a step back. Remind yourself of your unique strengths, experiences, and goals. Your journey is yours alone, and it's shaped by countless factors specific to you and your business. Instead of comparing yourself to others, try comparing your business to where it was a month ago, six months ago, or a year ago. This self-comparison is far more meaningful and motivating.

3. Celebrate small victories along the way

Did you land your first major client? Celebrate it. Did you figure out a more efficient way to run your operations? That's worth acknowledging. These small wins build confidence and remind you that you're making progress. Create a ritual for celebrating these victories - maybe treat your team to lunch, share your success with a mentor, or simply take a moment to feel proud of yourself and your business. By acknowledging these small achievements, you're training your brain to recognize progress and associate your efforts with positive outcomes. This positive reinforcement can help sustain your motivation during challenging times. Remember, big business accomplishments are often the result of many small victories strung together. By celebrating the small wins, you're building the resilience and confidence needed to achieve your larger entrepreneurial goals.

4. View Failures as Learning Opportunities

When something doesn't go as planned, ask yourself, "What can I learn from this? How can this make me stronger?" This mindset turns setbacks into stepping stones. Embrace the concept of "failing forward" - the idea that each failure brings you closer to success. After a setback, take time to reflect on what happened. Analyze the situation objectively, identifying factors within and outside your control. Consider keeping a "failure journal" where you document what went wrong, the lessons learned, and how you'll apply them in the future. This practice helps reframe failures as valuable experiences rather than defeats. Remember, many of the world's most successful people have stories of multiple failures before their breakthroughs. Your failures are not defining you; they're refining you.

5. Develop Problem-Solving Skills to Overcome Obstacle

Each challenge you face is an opportunity to become a better problem solver. Break big problems into smaller, manageable parts. Seek advice from others who have faced similar challenges. Start by clearly defining the problem at hand. Then, brainstorm multiple potential solutions without immediately judging their feasibility. Once you have a list of possible solutions, evaluate each one based on its potential effectiveness and your available resources. Don't be afraid to combine different ideas or to seek input from others.

The goal isn't to find a perfect solution but a workable one that

45

moves you forward. As you tackle each part of the problem, celebrate your progress. This approach not only makes big challenges less daunting but also builds your confidence in your ability to handle future obstacles.

Endurance is an essential principle for achieving lasting success in any venture. As I reflect on my journey in real estate, I recognize the challenges that have shaped me and the growth that has emerged from them. By embracing endurance, I have cultivated resilience, enabling me to rise above setbacks and maintain focus on my long-term vision.

In the world of entrepreneurship, where challenges are a constant, remember that endurance is not merely about surviving but thriving. It is the strength to rise, the resolve to persist, and the unwavering commitment to your goals that will carry you through even the most tumultuous storms. As you cultivate endurance, you equip yourself with the tools needed to not only maneuver through challenges but to emerge from them stronger, wiser, and more determined to succeed.

REFLECT AND ACT

1. How do you currently track and celebrate small victories in your entrepreneurial journey? Can you implement a new method to make this a regular practice?

2. In what ways do you practice self-care to maintain your mental and emotional strength? Are there any new self-care practices you'd like to incorporate?

3. What significant 90-day goal can you set for yourself? How will you break it down into weekly milestones and daily actions?

4. How can you ensure that self-care remains a priority amid your busy schedule?

5. What are the benefits of celebrating small victories, and how can this practice influence your team's morale?

6. How do you plan to balance short-term goals with your long-term vision?

7. What new self-care strategies can you explore to enhance your overall well-being?

Principle #4

EMBRACE CHANGE AND CULTIVATE FLEXIBILITY

"The art of life is a constant readjustment to our surroundings."

- KAKUZO OKAKURA

Embracing change and maintaining flexibility are vital principles for achieving lasting success in entrepreneurship. The business landscape is dynamic, constantly evolving, and often requiring swift adaptations to stay competitive. Embracing change means recognizing that evolution is inevitable and viewing it as a powerful opportunity for growth. Flexibility is the ability to adjust your strategies and approaches in response to these changes while keeping your overarching goals firmly in sight.

It doesn't mean compromising your core values or vision; rather, it involves being open to new ideas, learning from failures, and continuously innovating. This mindset allows entrepreneurs to maneuver through uncertainties, seize new opportunities, and sustain long-term success. As a Kikuyu

49

proverb from Kenya wisely states, "When the roots of a tree begin to decay, it spreads death to the branches" - underscoring the importance of staying adaptable and nurturing growth, even when faced with decay or challenges.

My journey in real estate was not a straight path but a winding road filled with unexpected turns. The challenges I encountered early on tested my ability to embrace change and stay flexible. One such instance was when the real estate market experienced a sudden downturn. This was a time of great uncertainty with fluctuating interest rates and hesitant buyers. The market slowed, and many real estate agents went two months or more without a sale, commission, or paycheck. Sales dropped, leaving full-time agents with little income potential. Many struggled to adapt, leading to many exits from the industry.

I recall vividly the day I realized I needed to pivot my strategy. I had several properties listed, but there were few inquiries, and the deals I was working on fell through. It was a disheartening period, but I knew that succumbing to the negativity around me would not solve the problem. Instead, I decided to look at the situation from a different perspective. What opportunities could this downturn present? How could I adapt my approach to meet the new market realities?

I began by increasing my focus on learning and professional development. I attended workshops and seminars that discussed strategies for surviving and thriving in a down market. I learned about creative financing options and alternative ways to add value to properties. This period of intensive learning not only equipped me with new tools but also reignited my passion for real estate.

One strategy that emerged was targeting a different segment of the market: rental properties. With many people hesitant to buy, the demand for rentals was on the rise. I shifted my focus to helping clients find rental properties and advising landlords on how to attract quality tenants. This pivot required me to learn about property management and the legalities involved in rentals, areas I had previously overlooked.

For instance, when Delaware shut down due to the COVID-19 pandemic, the real estate market faced unprecedented disruptions. People were fleeing big cities like New York and Philadelphia due to rising death tolls, adding layers of complexity to an already challenging market. During this time, I made a covenant with God, promising to give glory for every success in real estate. This spiritual commitment gave me strength and reinforced my growth mindset, encouraging me to persevere despite the uncertainties. I leveraged technology to enhance my services. I adopted virtual tour software and created detailed online listings with high-quality photos and videos. This approach catered to clients who were reluctant to visit properties in person, either due to market uncertainty or personal safety concerns. By offering a comprehensive virtual experience, I was able to maintain client engagement and interest.

The results were remarkable. Not only did my business

survive the downturn, but it also thrived in new ways. I built a reputation for being adaptable and innovative, which attracted a new clientele. My willingness to embrace change and remain flexible allowed me to turn a challenging situation into a growth opportunity.

As the market eventually recovered, I found myself better positioned than many of my peers. The skills and strategies I had developed during the downturn became invaluable assets. I continued to apply these lessons, always staying vigilant and ready to pivot as needed. This experience reinforced my belief that embracing change and maintaining flexibility are not just optional strategies but essential principles for long-term success.

Wangari Maathai's life also teaches us that flexibility and adaptability are not just survival tactics but are essential for creating lasting, meaningful impact. As the first African woman to receive the Nobel Peace Prize,[7] Maathai's accomplishments were rooted in her commitment to environmental conservation and women's rights. In 1977, she founded the Green Belt Movement, an initiative that began with the simple act of planting trees to combat deforestation in Kenya. However, the movement quickly evolved into a broader campaign that addressed issues of poverty, gender inequality, and environmental degradation.

---

7   "Wangari Maathai Facts," *The Nobel Peace Prize 2004*, The Nobel Prize, accessed August 25, 2024, https://www.nobelprize.org/prizes/peace/2004/maathai/facts/.

Maathai faced significant challenges along the way. Her activism put her at odds with powerful political forces in Kenya, leading to harassment, imprisonment, and even physical violence. Despite these obstacles, Maathai remained steadfast, continually adapting her strategies to navigate the shifting political landscape. She understood that to achieve her vision, she needed to be flexible, open to new approaches, and resilient in the face of adversity.

Her journey underscores that change, while often challenging, can serve as a powerful catalyst for growth and innovation.

Flexibility requires a willingness to pivot when necessary. This might mean altering your business model, updating your product offerings, or exploring new markets. During economic downturns or shifts in consumer behavior, a flexible entrepreneur reassesses their strategies and makes the necessary adjustments to remain viable. This agility becomes a competitive advantage, enabling sustained growth even in volatile environments.

Incorporating feedback from customers and stakeholders is another critical aspect of flexibility. By actively listening to your audience and responding to their needs, you can refine your products or services to better meet market demands. This customer-centric approach enhances satisfaction, builds loyalty, and drives long-term success.

Furthermore, fostering a culture of innovation within your organization encourages continuous improvement.

Encourage your team to experiment with new ideas and reward creative problem-solving. This can lead to breakthroughs that propel your business forward. Remember, some of the most successful companies started with a different idea and evolved through flexible thinking and adaptation.

Embracing change and maintaining flexibility requires strong leadership. Lead by example, demonstrating openness to new ideas and a readiness to adapt. Inspire your team to adopt the same mindset, fostering a collaborative environment where innovation thrives.

ADOPTING CHANGE FOR GROWTH

My journey in real estate has taught me that change can lead to growth. Embracing change is not merely about reacting to external pressures; it involves proactively seeking opportunities within those changes. When faced with market downturns, I learned to view challenges not as setbacks but as chances to pivot my strategy. This shift in perspective allowed me to remain agile, adapting my business model to meet the evolving needs of the market. By embracing change, we can uncover new paths to success.

Resilience is crucial for overcoming adversity in business. It is the backbone of enduring through difficult times and emerging stronger. In my real estate career, I encountered obstacles like fluctuating interest rates and hesitant buyers. Instead of giving up, I focused on learning from these experiences. Each setback became a lesson, prompting me to refine my techniques and enhance my understanding of the market. Building resilience helps entrepreneurs bounce back from setbacks and maintain momentum toward their goals. This relentless pursuit of improvement is essential for long-term success.

A strong focus on customer needs is vital for adapting to market changes. Understanding and responding to customer preferences can set businesses apart from the competition. During the pandemic, I recognized that many clients were reluctant to visit properties in person, so I created virtual tours to keep them engaged. These innovative solutions allowed me to maintain connections with clients, ensuring they still felt supported during uncertain times. By prioritizing customers, we can foster loyalty and drive innovation in our businesses.

HOW TO CULTIVATE A MINDSET THAT ADOPTS CHANGE AND FLEXIBILITY

1. Stay Curious

Curiosity is the cornerstone of continuous learning and growth. It pushes you to step outside your comfort zone, explore new ideas, and challenge the status quo. By fostering curiosity, you cultivate a mindset that is open to learning and innovation. Make it a habit to explore various industries and skills, even if they don't directly relate to your current job or expertise. Set aside time each week to delve into topics that intrigue you, whether through reading books, listening to podcasts, watching documentaries, or attending workshops.

For example, learning about digital marketing in your spare time might spark an interest in e-commerce or inspire a new strategy in your current field. This approach not only broadens your knowledge base but also enhances your creativity and problem-solving abilities. In a rapidly changing world, knowledge is a valuable currency, and curiosity is the key to accumulating it. The insights you gain today may become pivotal in solving tomorrow's challenges.

2. Be Open to Experimentation

Innovation thrives on experimentation, and a willingness to explore new approaches can lead to groundbreaking discoveries. Embrace the idea that life is a vast laboratory where every experience, regardless of its outcome, contributes to your growth and understanding. Start each day with the mindset that it's an opportunity to test a new idea or method. This experimental approach encourages you to take calculated risks, stepping outside your comfort zone to try something unfamiliar.

For instance, experimenting with a new project management tool or creative process can reveal more efficient ways to work, even if the initial attempts don't succeed. Viewing experimentation as a journey rather than a destination shifts your focus from the fear of failure to the value of learning. Over time, this mindset fosters adaptability, creativity, and resilience - essential traits for both entrepreneurship and personal development. By embracing experimentation, you develop the agility needed to thrive in a constantly changing environment.

3. View Change as an Opportunity

Change often triggers anxiety because it disrupts the stability we crave. However, learning to view change as an opportunity rather than a threat can significantly alter your approach to life's inevitable transitions. Start by acknowledging any fears or discomfort you feel when faced with change - recognizing these emotions is the first step toward overcoming them. Then, reframe your perspective by asking yourself, "What can I learn from this? How can this change help me grow?" Such reflective questioning allows you to uncover new insights about your capabilities and potential.

For example, a career shift may initially seem daunting, but it could also present opportunities to develop new skills, meet new people, or even rediscover passions you hadn't explored in years. By embracing change with a positive mindset, you transform challenges into stepping stones for both personal and professional development. Over time, this approach helps you build resilience and adaptability, key attributes for long-term success.

4. Develop Transferable Skills

In today's rapidly evolving job market, possessing a diverse skill set is increasingly valuable. While deep expertise in a specific area can be beneficial, developing transferable skills can provide greater flexibility and adaptability across different roles and industries. Transferable skills - such as communication, problem-solving, leadership, adaptability, emotional intelligence, and digital literacy - are valuable assets that can enhance your performance in various situations.

For instance, strong communication skills are essential whether you're leading a team, negotiating a deal, or presenting to stakeholders. Similarly, problem-solving abilities can help you navigate challenges across different contexts, while adaptability ensures you can quickly adjust to new circumstances. By focusing on building and refining these skills, you not only increase your marketability but also prepare yourself for a wider range of opportunities. In a world where change is the only constant, having a robust set of transferable skills positions you to thrive, no matter how the landscape shifts.

5. Network Across Industries

Your network is one of your most powerful resources, and its value increases when it spans multiple industries. While it's natural to gravitate toward connections within your field, branching out and building relationships across various industries can offer fresh perspectives, new opportunities, and invaluable support. Engaging with professionals from diverse backgrounds exposes you to different ways of thinking, challenges your assumptions, and broadens your understanding of how other sectors operate. Attend networking events, join professional associations, or participate in online forums that cater to a wide range of industries.

For example, a connection in the tech industry might introduce you to innovative tools that could streamline your operations, while a contact in finance could offer insights into managing your business's growth. A diverse network acts as a safety net when navigating career transitions or facing challenges, providing access to advice, mentorship, and opportunities that might not be available within your immediate circle. Remember, you never know where your next big idea or career breakthrough might come from - sometimes, it's from the most unexpected places.

By implementing these strategies, you can cultivate a mindset that embraces change and enhances your adaptability to new challenges. This approach empowers you to face uncertainties with confidence and resilience, setting the stage for continuous growth and long-term success. Embracing this mindset helps you seize opportunities, learn from experiences, and build a foundation for lasting achievement in both your personal and professional life.

REFLECT AND ACT

1. What recent changes in your industry or market have you noticed, and how can you adapt your business strategy to address them?

2. What transferable skills have you developed in your past experiences that you haven't fully utilized in your current

business? How can you integrate them?

3. How can you expand your network to include professionals from diverse industries, and what insights might you gain from them?

4. What innovative trends in other industries can you apply to your own business?

5. How do you stay updated on industry changes and ensure your strategies remain relevant?

6. What potential challenges do you foresee in your market, and how can you prepare for them?

7. How can you foster a culture of continuous learning and adaptation within your team?

Principle #5

NURTURE A GROWTH MINDSET FOR CONTINUOUS IMPROVEMENT

"The world is like a mask dancing. If you want to see it well, you do not stand in one place."

\- CHINUA ACHEBE,

At its core, a growth mindset stands in stark contrast to a fixed mindset, which assumes that qualities like intelligence and talent are static and unchangeable. Those with a growth mindset believe that effort and persistence can lead to improvement and success, even when faced with challenges and setbacks.

Embracing a growth mindset is a transformative approach that can profoundly influence your personal and professional development. Pioneered by psychologist Carol Dweck, this concept is based on the belief that one's abilities and intelligence can be developed through dedication, hard work, and continuous learning. As Dweck emphasizes, "The passion for stretching yourself and sticking to it, even (or especially) when it's not going well, is the hallmark of the growth mindset."8

For entrepreneurs, cultivating a growth mindset is especially crucial. The entrepreneurial journey is often riddled with obstacles, uncertainties, and failures. However, those who embrace this mindset see challenges as valuable opportunities for learning and growth, transforming potential barriers into stepping stones toward success.

My journey in real estate and entrepreneurship has been profoundly shaped by the growth mindset I cultivated over the years. This perspective has been instrumental in dealing with the complexities of the American business landscape and achieving long-term success.

As I continued to explore various business ventures, I realized that to truly succeed in America, I needed a deeper understanding of how the system worked. Education, I understood, was the key to unlocking many doors in this new world.

With this in mind, I decided to pursue a bachelor's degree

---

8   Carol S. Dweck, Mindset: The New Psychology of Success (New York: Random House, 2006), 14.

in organizational management. This choice was strategic - I aimed to become a business owner and a serial entrepreneur, and I knew this program would provide me with the knowledge and skills I needed.

Balancing full-time studies with my other commitments was no easy feat. There were many late nights of studying, early mornings of class attendance, and weekends spent on assignments. But with each course, I felt myself growing, and understanding more about the intricacies of American business culture.

In school, I began to understand how America functions, especially in the business sector. I learned about proposals and how to communicate effectively in a professional setting. These skills would prove invaluable in my future endeavors.

The classes on business strategy and entrepreneurship were particularly enlightening. They gave me a framework for understanding market dynamics, financial planning, and organizational behavior. As I absorbed this knowledge, I began to see opportunities everywhere. More importantly, it instilled in me the value of continuous learning and adaptability. I began to see each challenge not as a roadblock, but as an opportunity to expand my knowledge and skills.

A significant revelation in my journey came when I grappled with the weight of expectations -both self-imposed and external. Initially, these expectations often led to disappointment and frustration, creating unnecessary stress in my professional life. However, a breakthrough occurred when I decided to reframe my perspective on expectations.

I realized that eliminating the concept of "expectation" from my business relationships allowed me to focus on what truly mattered: my actions and personal growth. This shift in mindset was liberating. Instead of being preoccupied with how others might respond or what outcomes should occur, I concentrated on my principles, accountability, and personal development.

This new approach enabled me to maintain a clearer perspective in the face of challenges. I began to view setbacks not as failures, but as valuable learning experiences and stepping stones toward improvement. This resilience became a cornerstone of my entrepreneurial journey, allowing me to handle market fluctuations and adapt to changing circumstances with greater ease.

For instance, when I faced a significant downturn in the real estate market, instead of panicking or retreating, I saw it as a chance to learn more about market trends and consumer behavior. This shift in perspective led me to develop new strategies that ultimately strengthened my business, even during tough times.

The growth mindset also transformed how I approached feedback and criticism. Rather than viewing critiques as personal attacks, I began to see them as valuable inputs for improvement. This openness to feedback accelerated my learning curve and helped me refine my business strategies more effectively.

Moreover, this mindset shift had a profound impact on my leadership style. As I embraced continuous learning and personal growth, I found myself better equipped to inspire and motivate my team. I encouraged a culture of curiosity and resilience within my organization, which fostered innovation and adaptability. This approach reminds me of a proverb: "If you want to go fast, go alone. If you want to go far, go together." By cultivating a growth mindset not only in myself but in my team, I ensured that we all moved forward together, stronger and more united.

It has also influenced my approach to risk-taking in business. Instead of fearing potential failures, I began to see calculated risks as necessary steps in the entrepreneurial journey. This perspective allowed me to pursue opportunities that I might have previously avoided, leading to new avenues for business growth and personal development.

Another crucial aspect of a growth mindset has been the emphasis on continuous skill development. In the ever-evolving real estate market, staying relevant requires constant learning and adaptation. I made it a priority to stay informed about market trends, technological advancements, and changes in consumer behavior. This commitment to ongoing education has been instrumental in maintaining a competitive edge in the industry. It allowed me to adapt my strategies while thoroughly researching the market.

Early on, I realized that real estate goes far beyond selling properties. One major area is real estate investment, which offers wider opportunities. One option is becoming an investor yourself - buying properties to rent out, which can generate steady income even during tough market times. Another option is purchasing dilapidated homes, renovating them to modern standards, and selling them for a profit.

I invested my savings to gain hands-on experience in these areas. This not only brought in good profits but also gave me a deeper understanding of the buying and selling process for investment properties. After succeeding in rental properties and fix-and-flip ventures, I sought divine guidance to refine my strategy. My prayers for clarity were answered, and I developed a business strategy aimed at helping aspiring investors recognize the potential of real estate investing. This approach emphasized lifelong benefits, such as early retirement and financial sustainability.

Initially, it was challenging to convince seasoned investors to work with me, as many were loyal to their agents and teams. However, I trained a few new investors, guiding them to successfully fix and flip properties or purchase rental units based on their interests. It took time and dedication, but the results were impressive. These investors became successful, and many turned into loyal, repeat clients.

As my client base grew, these satisfied investors referred more than five friends or family members each, leading to even more transactions. This referral network became a steady stream of business, and my venture thrived.

I continually sharpened my real estate knowledge, learning new strategies to ensure my investors' continued success, which led to greater sales, referrals, and financial gains. I also became intentional about personal branding. I realized that my name, Jemimah Chuks, is a brand. This realization helped me stop playing small. I evolved, stood out, and competed at a high level.

Branding is more than just a logo or a business card. It's about the experience your clients associate with your name. Your brand should communicate who you are, what you stand for, and the value you bring. In my case, I positioned myself as someone investors could trust to help them succeed. By consistently delivering results, I built a personal brand that conveyed reliability, expertise, and value.

To grow your business, build a brand that stands out in your niche. Ask yourself: What makes me unique? Why should clients choose me over others? Once you've identified your unique selling points, ensure that everything you do reflects that. From your social media presence to how you interact with clients, consistency is key. A strong, authentic brand will not only attract clients but also keep them coming back and referring others.

The story of Philip Emeagwali, a renowned computer scientist from Southeastern Nigeria illustrates this principle. Emeagwali's journey is a testament to the transformative power of a growth mindset. Facing numerous obstacles, including limited resources and skepticism from the scientific community, Emeagwali's relentless pursuit of knowledge and innovation led him to develop groundbreaking techniques in supercomputing. His work earned him recognition as one of the most influential scientists of his time, demonstrating that perseverance and adaptability can turn challenges into significant achievements.[9]

Developing a growth mindset does not dismiss natural talents or innate abilities; rather, it recognizes that these qualities can be developed through hard work and experience. By adopting a growth mindset, entrepreneurs can push beyond perceived limitations, aiming for higher levels of achievement.

KEY COMPONENTS OF DEVELOPING A GROWTH MINDSET

1. Embracing Challenges

View the unique challenges you face every day as opportunities to learn and grow rather than as threats. When you encounter a market shift, a tough competitor, or a business obstacle, remind yourself that this is a chance to develop new skills and

---

9   "Philip Emeagwali," Computer Scientists of the African Diaspora, accessed August 25, 2024, https://www.math.buffalo.edu/mad/computer-science/emeagwali_philip.html.

knowledge. In such a difficult situation, instead of thinking, "I can't do this," try saying, "I can't do this yet, but I'm learning." This simple reframing can open up a world of possibilities. It acknowledges that you're on a journey of growth and that your current abilities are not the limit of your potential.

2. Persisting in the Face of Setbacks

Setbacks are an inevitable aspect of any entrepreneurial journey and should be viewed as opportunities rather than failures. Each challenge provides a chance to learn, adapt, and refine your approach. When you encounter a setback, remind yourself that it does not define your worth or capabilities but rather serves as a valuable lesson. Analyze what went wrong, identify areas for improvement, and apply these insights moving forward. This mindset not only fosters resilience but also enhances your problem-solving skills. Embracing setbacks with a positive outlook allows you to grow stronger and more adept at navigating future obstacles.

3. Valuing Effort

Hard work is key to achieving mastery. As an entrepreneur, you're familiar with putting in effort, but it's important to see this effort as valuable on its own, not just for the results it brings. Every hour spent learning new strategies, understanding market trends, or improving your skills is an investment in your growth. In Igbo culture, there's a saying, "O bu aka nri na-azo aka ekpe" (The right hand washes the left, and the left washes the right). This emphasizes the importance of effort and cooperation in achieving success. Embrace the process, knowing that your dedication builds the foundation for future success.

4. Learning from Criticism

In business, feedback on your product, service, or management style is common. Rather than becoming defensive, use this feedback to improve. View criticism as a valuable tool for enhancing your skills and adapting to your market. Remember the words of Nelson Mandela: "I never lose. I either win or learn." Criticism, when viewed through the lens of growth, is an opportunity to learn and grow, not a setback. Embrace it as an opportunity to learn and grow, which will help you refine your approach and succeed more effectively in your industry.

5. Finding Inspiration in Others' Success

Your entrepreneurial journey is unique, so avoid comparing yourself to others or feeling threatened by their achievements. Instead, draw inspiration from the successes of entrepreneurs within your industry. If someone has excelled in a particular skill or niche, study their journey to learn from their experiences. Their success demonstrates what's possible with dedication and hard work, and it can motivate you to push further. Remember, their accomplishments don't diminish your potential but highlight the opportunities available through perseverance and learning.

In entrepreneurship, a growth mindset serves as a powerful catalyst for innovation and problem-solving. It encourages creative thinking, experimentation with new approaches, and resilience in the face of initial failures - key ingredients for building and growing a successful business.

The influence of a growth mindset extends beyond individual performance. Entrepreneurs who embody this mindset can cultivate a culture of continuous improvement within their organizations, leading to enhanced innovation, adaptability to market changes, and improved team dynamics.

Moreover, a growth mindset shapes how entrepreneurs approach risk. Instead of viewing potential failures as definitive endpoints, those with a growth mindset see them as valuable learning experiences. This perspective fosters calculated risk-taking and a willingness to explore uncharted territories in business.

Embracing a growth mindset also aligns with the notion of lifelong learning, which is essential for success in the fast-paced, ever-evolving business landscape. Entrepreneurs who adopt this mindset are more likely to stay abreast of industry trends, emerging technologies, and shifting market demands.

VALUABLE INSIGHTS GAINED

As I reflect on my journey, I realize that the growth mindset was not just a tool for overcoming challenges but a way of life that continuously propelled me toward my goals. This mindset allowed me to adapt, evolve, and thrive in an environment where many would have given up.

By embracing a growth mindset, I've managed uncertainties with confidence and creativity. Continuous education emerges as a vital component, providing a deeper understanding of the business environment and proving invaluable for strategic decision-making and long-term success. Investing in ongoing training and professional development equips me with the tools necessary to respond effectively to market changes.

By shifting focus to actions and personal growth rather than external and self-imposed pressures, I found that I could maintain clarity and reduce stress. This approach enables me to prioritize what truly matters, allowing for a balanced perspective on both successes and setbacks. This approach allows for a profound shift in perspective, where setbacks become valuable learning experiences rather than failures, thereby enhancing resilience. I learned that each challenge presents an opportunity to adapt and grow, fostering a more positive outlook on my journey.

The importance of welcoming feedback and criticism cannot be overstated. Viewing critiques as opportunities for improvement rather than personal attacks accelerates growth and refines business strategies. By soliciting feedback actively and integrating it into my decision-making process, I have seen tangible improvements in my performance and the overall effectiveness of my team. This openness to feedback cultivates a culture of continuous improvement within an organization, driving innovation and adaptability.

A growth mindset significantly impacts leadership. By prioritizing continuous learning and personal development, I encourage a culture of curiosity, resilience, and innovation within my teams. This emphasis on growth not only boosts morale but also fosters collaboration and creativity, leading to better overall performance and increased adaptability in the face of challenges.

Adopting a proactive approach to risk-taking emerges as an essential lesson. Viewing calculated risks as necessary steps in the entrepreneurial journey allows for the pursuit of new opportunities and drives business growth. This forward-thinking mindset, coupled with an emphasis on continuous skill development and staying informed about industry trends, helps maintain a competitive edge in a dynamic business environment.

HOW TO CULTIVATE A GROWTH MINDSET

1. Reframe Your Thoughts

Monitor your self-talk and consciously replace fixed mindset phrases with growth-oriented ones. Instead of saying, "I can't understand this market," say, "I'm learning more about this market every day." When you catch yourself thinking, "I'll never be as successful as my competitors," reframe it to, "I'm developing the skills and knowledge to become a successful entrepreneur in this industry." This shift in perspective helps you embrace challenges as opportunities for growth rather than viewing them as insurmountable obstacles. By consistently practicing this reframing technique, you create a positive mental environment that encourages resilience and motivation in the face of adversity.

2. Set Learning Goals

In addition to your business achievement goals, establish specific learning objectives. For example, if you're aiming to expand your business, a related learning goal might be to understand a new market segment or master a new technology. Break these learning goals into small, manageable steps and celebrate each step completed. Instead of focusing solely on what you want to achieve - such as a certain revenue level, market share, or product launch - consider what you want to learn along the way. This dual focus enriches your journey and enhances your understanding, making the process rewarding regardless of the outcome, and allows you to build a robust foundation for future success.

3. Celebrate the Process

Acknowledge your efforts and progress, not just the results. At the end of each week, reflect on what you've learned and how you've grown. Did you have a productive meeting with a potential investor today, even if they didn't commit? Did you manage a complex regulatory issue? Did you learn a new business skill, even if you haven't mastered it yet? These are all wins worth celebrating. By cultivating a habit of recognizing these small victories, you reinforce a positive mindset that encourages continuous growth and motivation, which helps you stay focused on your long-term objectives while enjoying the journey.

4. Cultivate Curiosity

Embrace your business environment with a sense of genuine curiosity. Ask questions about industry trends, new technologies, and market dynamics. Strive to understand not just the what but also the why behind these elements. This approach will enhance your ability to learn and adapt quickly. Additionally, your curiosity will make you more appealing to potential partners and customers, who will value your sincere interest in their needs and perspectives. By fostering a culture of curiosity within your organization, you can inspire your team to innovate and explore new solutions, driving overall success and engagement.

5. Practice Self-Reflection

Regularly evaluate your growth and learning experiences. Dedicate time each week to reflect on what you've learned, the challenges you've encountered, and how you've evolved. Keeping a journal can help you track your progress over time. Ask yourself questions such as: What new skills have I developed this month? How have I adjusted my business strategies based on my learning? What ongoing challenges am I facing, and how can I approach them differently? This structured self-reflection process enables you to gain insights into your development, identify areas for improvement, and set informed goals for the future, reinforcing your commitment to personal and professional growth.

Building on this reflection fosters continuous development and adaptability. With a growth mindset, every challenge becomes an opportunity, every setback a lesson, and every effort a step toward mastery. Your potential as an entrepreneur isn't fixed; it's an ever-expanding landscape of possibilities waiting to be explored.

REFLECT AND ACT

1. What fixed mindset thoughts did you have today? How can you reframe each of these with a growth mindset perspective?

2. What was your most recent setback? What did you learn from it, and how can you apply this lesson moving forward?

3. Which skill do you want to improve over the next 30 days? How can you focus on the process of learning rather than the result?

4. How can you create a habit of reflecting on your mindset regularly to encourage growth?

5. What role does resilience play in your approach to overcoming setbacks?

6. How do you plan to celebrate progress in your skill development journey?

7. What strategies can you implement to maintain a growth mindset in challenging situations?

Principle #6

MASTER EMOTIONAL INTELLIGENCE

===

"The greatest ability in business is to get along with others and to influence their actions."

- JOHN HANCOCK

Entrepreneurship can be challenging, regardless of your background. One key skill that can significantly contribute to your success is emotional intelligence (EQ). This involves understanding and managing your own emotions, as well as recognizing and influencing the emotions of others. Mastering EQ helps you build stronger relationships, manage complex business situations, and excel in diverse environments.

Cultivating emotional intelligence is crucial for entrepreneurs. Beyond managing a business, you need to connect with clients, employees, and partners from varied backgrounds and cultures. Every industry and market has its own unwritten rules about emotions and behavior. Emotional intelligence enables you to manage these nuances effectively. By being attuned to the emotional dynamics within your business, you can foster a more cohesive and motivated team. Employees are more likely to feel valued and understood, leading to higher productivity and job satisfaction.

Real estate has taught me the invaluable role of emotional intelligence and empathy in building lasting relationships with clients and colleagues. Early in my career, I realized that success was not just about closing deals but about understanding and connecting with people on a deeper level. This insight came to me during a particularly challenging time when I was trying to secure a deal with a client who was hesitant and indecisive.

This client had recently moved to the United States and was unfamiliar with the real estate market. They were anxious about making the right decision for their family. Recognizing their anxiety, I decided to take a different approach. Instead of pushing for a quick sale, I spent time listening to their concerns and understanding their needs. I empathized with their situation, recalling my own experiences of getting used to new environments and making significant decisions.

I took the time to educate them about the market, patiently answering all their questions and addressing their fears. This approach not only eased their anxiety but also built a strong foundation of trust. Eventually, they felt confident enough to make an informed decision, and the deal went through smoothly. This experience reinforced the importance of empathy and emotional intelligence in my business interactions.

Another instance where emotional intelligence played a crucial role was during the COVID-19 pandemic. With the market in turmoil and clients facing unprecedented uncertainty, it was essential to maintain composure and offer reassurance. I made a conscious effort to stay connected with my clients, offering support and understanding. Whether it was through virtual consultations or regular check-ins, I prioritized their emotional well-being alongside their real estate needs.

This period also tested my self-awareness and self-regulation. With the pressure mounting and the future uncertain, I had to manage my own emotions effectively to remain a stable and reliable resource for my clients. By practicing mindfulness and staying attuned to my emotional state, I was able to maintain a positive outlook and provide the necessary guidance and support.

Earlier in my business, I struggled with interactions at networking events and professional settings. I was ambitious and driven, but I lacked the emotional intelligence to understand the nuances of business relationships effectively. I often found myself frustrated with what I perceived as inefficiency or lack of vision in others, not realizing that my behavior was hindering my progress.

I remember one particular industry conference where I approached potential partners with great enthusiasm about my ideas. I would launch into detailed explanations of my business plan, saying things like, "Your approach is outdated. Here's how you should be doing it instead." I didn't realize that this direct, almost aggressive style, which might have been acceptable in my previous work environment, was seen as arrogant and off-putting in this new context.

Over time, I've come to understand that business success isn't just about having great ideas; it's about how you communicate those ideas and build relationships. I've learned that people have different perspectives shaped by their own experiences, and it's not my place to dictate how they should think or operate their businesses.

This realization has been transformative in my professional relationships. I've learned to communicate more thoughtfully, considering the feelings and perspectives of others before I speak. Now, instead of telling people what to do, I ask questions about their businesses, listen to their challenges, and offer suggestions more collaboratively.

I also understood the importance of adapting my communication style to connect with different types of professionals. Just as a skilled salesperson tailors their pitch to different customers, entrepreneurs need to adjust their approach based on their audience. This doesn't mean compromising your vision or values; rather, it's about finding common ground and building understanding.

For example, when pitching to investors now, I focus on the aspects of my business that align with their interests and investment strategies. When collaborating with other entrepreneurs, I emphasize mutual benefits and shared challenges. This approach has not only improved my business relationships but has also opened doors to opportunities I might have missed with my earlier, less emotionally intelligent approach.

COMPONENTS OF EMOTIONAL INTELLIGENCE

1. Self-awareness

Self-awareness is the foundation of emotional intelligence. It encompasses the ability to recognize and understand your emotions, thoughts, and motivations. It involves introspection, allowing you to identify your strengths and weaknesses, which is crucial for personal and professional growth. When you're self-aware, you can better gauge how your feelings influence your business decisions, leadership style, and interactions with others. This insight empowers you to make more informed choices, cultivate authentic relationships, and respond to challenges with clarity and purpose. Ultimately, self-awareness fosters a sense of authenticity that resonates with clients and employees alike.

2. Self-regulation

Self-regulation refers to your ability to manage and control your emotions, particularly in high-pressure business situations. It does not imply suppressing feelings but rather recognizing them and choosing how to respond constructively. Practicing self-regulation allows you to remain calm and composed during conflicts or crises, fostering rational decision-making instead of reactive behavior. This skill is vital for maintaining professionalism and credibility in your entrepreneurial endeavors. By cultivating self-regulation, you can approach challenges with a clear mind, making thoughtful choices that contribute to your long-term success and the well-being of your team.

3. Motivation

Motivation is a key aspect of emotional intelligence that drives you toward achieving your business goals. It involves harnessing your emotions to maintain a positive attitude and perseverance, even in the face of adversity. Individuals with strong motivation are not easily discouraged by setbacks; instead, they view challenges as opportunities for growth. This intrinsic drive not only propels your progress but also inspires those around you. By fostering motivation within yourself and your team, you create a culture of resilience and determination, ensuring that everyone remains focused on collective objectives, even when obstacles arise.

4. Empathy

"Empathy is the ability to read emotions in others."[10] It entails putting yourself in someone else's shoes, whether a customer, employee, or business partner, to better grasp their feelings and perspectives. Empathy allows you to connect on a deeper level, fostering trust and collaboration in your business relationships.

---

10   Daniel Goleman, Emotional Intelligence: Why It Can Matter More Than IQ (1995; repr., London: Bloomsbury, 2009), 10.

By practicing empathy, you can enhance communication, address concerns effectively, and build a supportive work environment. This skill is essential for resolving conflicts and cultivating loyalty among clients and employees, ultimately contributing to a more harmonious and productive workplace.

5. Social skills

Social skills cover the ability to build and maintain positive relationships, communicate effectively, and collaborate with others. This includes the capacity to work well in a team, resolve conflicts amicably, and influence others positively. Strong social skills enable you to navigate various business situations, from networking events to team meetings, fostering a sense of camaraderie and cooperation. By honing your social skills, you enhance your ability to connect with diverse individuals, create lasting partnerships, and lead your team with confidence. Ultimately, effective social skills contribute to a thriving business environment where everyone can succeed together.

In today's globalized business world, where diversity is increasingly valued, your ability to understand and relate to people from various backgrounds can become your greatest asset. It can make it easier to build a strong network, create a positive company culture, and ultimately lead to a more fulfilling and successful entrepreneurial journey. Additionally, being emotionally intelligent allows you to handle stress and setbacks with greater resilience. When faced with challenges, you can maintain a calm and focused demeanor, making it easier to find solutions and keep your team motivated.

The journey of Ngozi Okonjo-Iweala, Nigeria's former Finance Minister, illustrates the power of emotional intelligence and empathy. Her ability to navigate complex political and economic landscapes, gain respect globally, and become the first woman to head the World Trade Organization, exemplifies how these skills can drive success. Okonjo-Iweala's approach, grounded in empathy and emotional understanding, aligns with the Igbo proverb that says, "A child who washes his hands clean will eat with elders," emphasizing the importance of humility, respect, and empathy in gaining wisdom and influence.

Embracing emotional intelligence and empathy has been transformative in my journey. These skills have not only helped me understand complex business environments but have also enabled me to build meaningful and lasting relationships. As I continue to grow, I remain committed to fostering a culture of understanding and connection, knowing that these qualities are key to enduring success.

HOW TO CULTIVATE EMOTIONAL INTELLIGENCE

1. Develop Self-Awareness

Self-awareness is the foundation of emotional intelligence, and it begins with a deep understanding of your own emotions, strengths, and weaknesses. By regularly reflecting on your emotional responses and how they influence your behavior and decision-making, you can become more attuned to your inner self. Start by keeping a daily journal where you record your emotional experiences and reactions to different situations. This practice will help you identify patterns, triggers, and recurring themes over time.

For instance, you might notice that certain types of feedback trigger anxiety or defensiveness, which can then inform how you approach similar situations in the future. Additionally, consider seeking the guidance of a mentor or coach who can offer objective insights and help you gain a deeper understanding of your emotional landscape. Engaging in mindfulness practices, such as meditation or deep breathing exercises, can also enhance your self-awareness by keeping you grounded in the present moment.

2. Practice Self-Regulation

Self-regulation is the ability to manage your emotions, especially in stressful or challenging situations. It allows you to respond to difficulties thoughtfully, rather than reacting impulsively. To cultivate self-regulation, start by incorporating short mindfulness exercises into your daily routine. For example, practicing mindful breathing or progressive muscle relaxation can help you stay calm and centered, even amid pressure. During high-stress moments, take a brief pause to collect your thoughts before responding. This intentional pause can prevent rash decisions and promote more measured, effective actions.

Additionally, journaling your emotions can be a powerful tool for processing your feelings and maintaining emotional balance. Regular self-care activities, such as exercise, hobbies, or spending quality time with loved ones, are also crucial for emotional regulation. These activities help recharge your emotional reserves and keep you grounded, enabling you to handle challenges with greater resilience and poise.

3. Enhance Your Empathy

Empathy, the ability to understand and share the feelings of others, is a crucial component of emotional intelligence. It fosters trust and strengthens relationships, which are vital for successful business interactions. To enhance your empathy, make a conscious effort to practice active listening. This means giving your full attention to the speaker, avoiding interruptions, and reflecting on what you've heard to ensure understanding. Ask open-ended questions to encourage deeper conversations and show genuine interest in the experiences and perspectives of others. Engage in perspective-taking exercises where you imagine yourself in someone else's situation to better appreciate their viewpoint.

For example, if a colleague seems stressed, consider the pressures they might be facing, and offer support accordingly. Additionally, seek out diverse experiences and interactions that broaden your understanding of different cultures, backgrounds, and emotional responses. This exposure will deepen your empathy and help you connect with others on a more meaningful level.

4. Improve Your Social Skills

Strong social skills are essential for building and maintaining positive relationships with clients, colleagues, and partners. These skills include effective communication, conflict resolution, and teamwork, all of which are critical in a professional setting. To improve your social skills, practice active listening by paying close attention to others when they speak, and respond thoughtfully. Clear articulation of your ideas is also important, so work on expressing yourself in a way that is concise and easily understood.

Collaborative problem-solving is another key aspect; focus on fostering a positive and inclusive environment where everyone feels their contributions are valued. Attending workshops or training sessions on communication and interpersonal skills can further enhance your abilities. Additionally, nonverbal communication, such as maintaining eye contact and using appropriate body language, plays a significant role in building rapport. By refining these social skills, you'll be better equipped to navigate complex interactions and foster strong, productive relationships.

5. Seek Feedback and Reflect

Continuous learning and adaptation are vital for enhancing your emotional intelligence (EQ) and becoming a more effective leader or entrepreneur. Regularly seeking feedback from others about your emotional intelligence and empathy is a key step in this process. Establish a routine for soliciting feedback from trusted mentors, peers, or team members, and create an action plan based on their insights. This feedback loop allows you to identify blind spots and areas for improvement. Engage in self-reflection exercises where you assess your progress and set specific, measurable goals for your development.

For instance, if feedback indicates that you need to improve your conflict resolution skills, you can focus on learning techniques to manage disagreements more effectively. Additionally, participating in peer support groups or networking events where you can exchange experiences with others can provide valuable perspectives on emotional intelligence. This ongoing process of feedback and reflection will help you continually refine your EQ and enhance your effectiveness in both personal and professional settings.

By developing your emotional intelligence, you'll gain a deeper understanding of the complexities of the business world. This enhancement will enable you to build stronger relationships with clients, employees, and partners while equipping you to handle the emotional challenges of entrepreneurship. As you continue to practice these skills, you'll discover how they enrich your entrepreneurial journey, making it both more rewarding and successful.

REFLECT AND ACT

1. Think of a challenging person in your professional life. How can you use perspective-taking to better understand their point of view?

2. Which culture different from your own can you learn about this week? How might this experience change your perspective and enhance your cultural empathy?

3. Who are three people you trust who could give you honest feedback on your interpersonal skills? What specific areas will you ask them about, and how will you use this feedback to grow?

4. How can you foster a more inclusive environment within your team or organization?

5. What strategies can you use to improve your active listening skills in professional interactions?

6. How do you plan to incorporate feedback into your personal and professional development?

7. What role does empathy play in enhancing your leadership capabilities?

Principle #7

NETWORK AND COLLABORATE EFFECTIVELY

"Alone we can do so little; together we can do so much."

- HELEN KELLER

Success rarely happens in isolation. As entrepreneurs, we often feel the pressure to prove ourselves on our own. However, building relationships, networking, and forming partnerships are essential steps on the road to achieving our goals. Effective networking and collaboration can provide access to new opportunities and resources, offer diverse perspectives and ideas, create a support system during challenging times, and enhance your visibility and credibility in your field.

"A single tree does not make a forest," they say. Joining eXp Realty marked a significant turning point in my career. Attending national events, I had the opportunity to meet agents who were selling 200 to 300 homes annually. Initially, this seemed beyond my reach, but as I listened to their stories and strategies, I realized they were ordinary people, much like you and me. This realization was profound; it expanded my horizons and ignited my imagination. I saw that I, too, could achieve more than I had ever dreamed possible. That's the power of networking.

Before attending these events, I had set a goal to sell 50 homes in 2020. However, after meeting these high-performing agents, I understood I had been thinking too small. Their success stories inspired me to dream bigger and adopt similar systems in my work. This shift in perspective was a game-changer.

Hearing about their methods and the tools they used, I started implementing new strategies and leveraging technology more effectively. I began to see the value of streamlined processes and the importance of building a strong support network. These insights allowed me to optimize my workflow and enhance my productivity.

One of the most valuable lessons I learned was the importance of perseverance and consistency. These top agents had faced numerous challenges and setbacks, yet their determination and resilience kept them moving forward. Their stories taught me that success is not about avoiding failures but about learning from them and continuing to push through obstacles.

Moreover, the power of collaboration and sharing knowledge within the eXp Realty community was incredibly motivating. The culture of support and encouragement fostered an environment where agents could thrive. By participating in mastermind sessions and networking events, I gained access to a wealth of experience and expertise that helped me refine my approach to real estate.

Inspired by these interactions, I set new, more ambitious goals for myself. I aimed to not only match the achievements of these top agents but to also surpass them. This renewed sense of purpose and direction had a transformative effect on my business. I began to see significant growth in my sales and an increase in client satisfaction.

You might be wondering, "That's great, but how does this apply to me?" The principles of networking and collaboration are universal and relevant across all industries. Building effective networks can open doors you never knew existed, providing access to new opportunities and diverse perspectives. Additionally, these connections create a support system during challenging times and enhance your visibility and credibility in your field. A strong network and solid business partnerships are essential for establishing an effective system. Collaboration ensures that everyone contributes their part, facilitating smooth operations and success, regardless of whether you're in tech, retail, services, or any other sector.

When you network and collaborate, you're not just benefiting from others; you're also contributing your unique insights. This exchange of ideas and experiences can lead to innovation and growth that benefits everyone involved. By actively engaging in networking and collaboration, you can unlock new possibilities, build meaningful relationships, and drive success in your endeavors.

The impact of networking and collaboration became clear to me early in my career when my curiosity and passion for media and communication grew stronger. This enthusiasm paved the way for an exciting endeavor – the creation of "The Jemimah Show." The idea for the show came from a desire to create a platform for people of color's voices to be heard. I aimed to bring stories of immigrants, entrepreneurs, and everyday heroes to the forefront. It was an ambitious project, especially for someone with no prior experience in television production.

We faced fierce competition from established talk shows, but I was determined to stand out. We committed to delivering content that was not only entertaining but also deeply impactful. I spent countless hours researching topics, vetting guests, and crafting questions that would lead to meaningful conversations. This often meant working late nights and weekends, but the results were transformative. We operated on a shoestring budget, often improvising solutions to technical problems. I remember using bedsheets as makeshift backdrops and borrowing equipment from friends. But what we lacked in resources, we made up for in passion and creativity.

Our first few episodes were far from perfect. I stumbled over my words, forgot questions, and struggled with the timing.

Yet, with each episode, I grew more confident. I learned to connect with guests and draw out their stories in a way that was engaging and authentic. As word of the show spread, our viewership began to grow. We became known for discussions that truly resonated with our audience. We tackled topics that other shows shied away from - the challenges of immigration, the struggles of starting a business, and the complexities of cultural identity in America.

We went above and beyond in our audience engagement, personally responding to every message we received and organizing regular meet-and-greets. This commitment to excellence and our audience built a loyal fan base that stayed with us throughout the show's run. Hosting "The Jemimah Show" imparted invaluable lessons in leadership, innovation, and the significance of connecting with people. It demonstrated that with passion and commitment, one can create something meaningful despite the odds.

The show's success opened doors I never imagined possible. I had the opportunity to interview several senators in Delaware, the governor, and numerous ambassadors in D.C. These experiences not only broadened my network but also reinvigorated my passion for politics and social issues. As I built relationships with clients and colleagues in the real estate sector, I saw firsthand the impact of collaboration, creating opportunities, fostering connections, and driving personal and professional growth.

Networking transcends the simple act of exchanging business cards or attending industry events; it's about fostering genuine connections that lead to collaborative ventures. Each interaction holds growth potential, as engaging with others allows us to tap into their wealth of knowledge and experience. This exchange of ideas can lead to fresh insights that may not have been possible in isolation.

Collaboration further amplifies this potential by uniting individuals toward common objectives. It recognizes the value of shared resources, skills, and insights, demonstrating that we can accomplish more collectively than we can alone. By pooling our talents, we can develop innovative solutions that drive greater success for all parties involved.

The Igbo Apprenticeship System is a prime example of this principle in action. This traditional system underscores the power of collaboration by having seasoned entrepreneurs mentor and support younger ones. Many of Nigeria's most successful businessmen have emerged through this network-based approach, showcasing how deep, supportive connections and collaborative efforts can profoundly influence success.

Reid Hoffman's journey offers another brilliant illustration of networking and collaboration's transformative power. Imagine this: LinkedIn's story began with Hoffman envisioning a platform where professionals could connect and advance their careers. He didn't just create a website; he built a thriving community. Hoffman's knack for networking was crucial; he reached out to investors who believed in his vision, securing the initial funding necessary to launch LinkedIn.

Hoffman's approach to collaboration was equally noteworthy. He encouraged a culture within LinkedIn that valued teamwork and innovation. Employees were empowered to share ideas and collaborate across departments, leading to rapid growth and the introduction of new features that enhanced user experience. Strategic partnerships with other companies further extended LinkedIn's capabilities, demonstrating how collaborative efforts can drive a company's success.

The lessons from Hoffman's story highlight the significance of building and leveraging a strong network. His ability to connect with others and forge meaningful relationships was pivotal in LinkedIn's rise to becoming the world's largest professional networking site. His journey serves as a powerful reminder that networking and collaboration are essential components of entrepreneurial success.

Ultimately, networking and collaboration create a vibrant ecosystem that supports entrepreneurial growth. This interconnectedness fosters a culture of learning and improvement, where individuals uplift one another and inspire each other to push beyond perceived limitations. Embracing the power of collaboration can transform our entrepreneurial journeys, leading to breakthroughs that might otherwise remain unattainable.

THE POWER OF CONNECTIONS

Through my experiences, I learned that effective networking and collaboration can significantly enhance your entrepreneurial journey. It's not just about what you can gain; it's about the value you can provide to others. Every interaction is an opportunity to share knowledge, learn from others, and cultivate meaningful relationships. By focusing on giving rather than receiving, you foster an environment where others feel encouraged to share their insights and expertise, creating a mutually beneficial cycle of support. The more you engage with people, the more you realize that collaboration leads to innovation and growth. When you approach networking with a mindset of generosity and a willingness to help others, you create a supportive ecosystem where everyone can thrive, ultimately driving collective success and progress.

Furthermore, I discovered that seeking out mentors and coaches is crucial for personal and professional development. These individuals can guide you, share their experiences, and help you manage challenges. Mentors often provide a roadmap, helping you handle industry complexities based on their journeys. They can offer insights that you might not have considered, suggesting strategies that align with your goals while also highlighting potential pitfalls. Their guidance can be invaluable in avoiding common mistakes and accelerating your growth. Investing in mentorship can lead to transformative experiences that shape your trajectory, ultimately helping you achieve your aspirations more efficiently.

Networking isn't solely about formal events; it's about being open to connections in everyday life. Casual conversations, chance encounters, and even online interactions can lead to significant opportunities. For instance, a brief chat with a stranger at a coffee shop or a comment on a social media post can spark a connection that leads to a partnership or collaboration. You never know where a simple chat might lead, so remain approachable and open to new connections. This openness can create unexpected pathways, enabling you to discover new avenues for growth and innovation that you may not have previously considered.

Additionally, I learned the importance of active listening in networking. Truly listening to others, understanding their needs, and offering genuine support can build trust and deepen relationships. Active listening involves engaging with empathy, asking thoughtful questions, and reflecting on what others share. This trust forms the foundation of strong, lasting connections that can benefit both parties. By cultivating a habit of attentive listening, you enhance your ability to foster deeper relationships, enabling you to collaborate more effectively and leverage each other's strengths to achieve common goals. Ultimately, building a network based on trust and mutual support creates a powerful foundation for personal and professional success.

HOW TO NETWORK AND COLLABORATE

1. Be Genuine in Your Interactions

Authenticity is essential when building your network. You lay a foundation for meaningful relationships when you approach others with a sincere interest in their work and experience. Focus on fostering connections rather than merely advancing your agenda. Take the time to learn about others' passions and motivations by asking thoughtful questions that encourage dialogue. Show genuine curiosity about their journeys and listen actively to their responses. This kind of engagement builds trust and establishes a rapport that can lead to more fruitful connections and collaborations.

Remember, people are more likely to engage with you if they sense your interest is genuine. By being open, honest, and transparent in your interactions, you create an inviting atmosphere that encourages reciprocity. Your willingness to invest time in understanding others can set the foundation for a robust and supportive network, enhancing both your personal and professional life.

2. Attend Networking Events

Actively seek out industry-specific events, conferences, and workshops to meet like-minded individuals and expand your network. Engaging in face-to-face conversations allows you to establish connections, share experiences, and gain insights from fellow attendees. To maximize these opportunities, prepare an elevator pitch that succinctly introduces who you are, what you do, and what makes you unique. Utilize these gatherings to connect with speakers and participants, as you may discover valuable relationships that could lead to future collaborations.

After the event, don't forget to follow up with those you met, reinforcing the connection and expressing appreciation for their time. Networking events are not only essential for expanding your professional network but also for creating lasting relationships that can unlock new opportunities and avenues for growth. By immersing yourself in these settings, you cultivate an environment ripe for mutual support and collaboration.

3. Leverage Online Platforms

Utilize social media platforms like LinkedIn, Twitter, and Facebook to expand your professional network effectively. By engaging with others online, you can share valuable content, comment on relevant posts, and participate in discussions that resonate with your field. Building an online presence enhances your credibility and visibility while connecting you with a broader audience. Don't hesitate to reach out to professionals whose work inspires you, as many are open to connecting and sharing insights.

Use these platforms to showcase your expertise, post about your projects, and engage in conversations that demonstrate your knowledge and passion. Additionally, consider joining industry-specific groups or forums where you can interact with others who share your interests and challenges. Remember, online networking is just as vital as in-person interactions in today's digital age. By actively participating in these communities, you create opportunities for collaboration and mentorship that can enrich your professional journey.

4. Seek Mentorship

Identifying individuals who inspire you and reaching out for mentorship opportunities can significantly enhance your career. A mentor can provide invaluable guidance, constructive feedback, and emotional support as you navigate your entrepreneurial journey. When seeking mentorship, be clear about what you hope to achieve and specify the areas where you seek guidance, whether it is strategic planning, marketing, or work-life balance. This clarity helps mentors understand how best to assist you and fosters a productive relationship. Do not hesitate to ask for advice or share your goals with them; openness fosters trust. Cultivating a mentor-mentee relationship can provide insights into challenges you have yet to face, allowing you to learn from their experiences. The wisdom and insights of your mentor can accelerate your growth and help you avoid common pitfalls in your career. Ultimately, mentorship can be a transformative experience, equipping you with the tools you need to succeed.

5. Collaborate on Projects

Look for opportunities to collaborate with others in your field to maximize creativity and innovation. Partnering on projects can lead to fresh perspectives and unique solutions that benefit both parties - approach potential collaborators with well-defined ideas about how you can work together to achieve mutual goals. Whether through joint ventures, community initiatives, or co-hosting events, collaboration enables you to pool resources, knowledge, and expertise, enhancing the overall outcome. Open communication is essential to ensure that both parties align on objectives and expectations.

Remember, collaboration is about leveraging each other's strengths to achieve results that would be challenging to attain alone. By collaborating, you not only foster a sense of camaraderie but also create a support system that encourages growth and development. The relationships forged through collaborative efforts can lead to lasting professional connections, expanding your network and increasing your influence in your industry.

Networking and collaboration are essential for success in any entrepreneurial journey. By fostering genuine relationships and embracing teamwork, you can create a supportive ecosystem that propels you toward your goals. Networking is not solely about what you can gain; it's also about the value you provide to others. Engaging with your network and working collaboratively will open doors to new opportunities, offer fresh perspectives, and unlock potential for innovation and growth. Embrace the power of connection and collaboration, and watch your efforts propel you toward success.

REFLECT AND ACT

1. Who are three new professional connections you aim to make this month? What's your plan to meet them?

2. How could you organize a small gathering that brings together professionals from diverse backgrounds? What insights might you gain from this experience?

3. What collaboration ideas can you brainstorm that leverage your unique background? Who could you reach out to discuss these ideas?

4. How can you strengthen your existing professional relationships to foster mutual growth?

5. What networking opportunities can you explore to expand your industry connections?

6. How do you plan to maintain and nurture the new connections you make?

7. What collaborative projects can you initiate to leverage the strengths of your network?

Principle #8

UNLEASH YOUR CONFIDENCE AND BE POSITIVE

"With confidence, you have won before you have started."

- MARCUS GARVEY

With my license in hand, I was ready to take on the real estate world. However, the challenges were far from over. When I proudly announced my new status as a realtor to the woman who had initially guided me, her response was less than encouraging. "But you're pregnant," she said. "People who aren't pregnant haven't even sold a house, let alone a pregnant lady."

Her words could have been discouraging, but I chose to see them as a challenge. I replied with conviction, "Give me a chance, and I will show you who I am. Just give me a chance." Her skeptical "Well, we'll see" only fueled my determination to succeed.

Early in my career, I faced a significant challenge that tested my confidence and positivity. It was my first year in the real estate industry, and I had just secured a listing for a beautiful, high-end property in a competitive market. This was a major opportunity for me, but it was also incredibly intimidating. The stakes were high, and the client had very high expectations. As a relatively new agent, I was still building my reputation and learning the ropes. I knew that selling this property could be a game-changer for my career, but the pressure was immense. I had moments of self-doubt, wondering if I was really up to the task. However, I decided to face the challenge with confidence and a positive attitude.

First, I focused on preparation. I researched the market thoroughly, studied comparable properties, and developed a comprehensive marketing strategy. I made sure I was knowledgeable about every detail of the property and its unique selling points. This preparation gave me the confidence to speak authoritatively about the property to potential buyers and other agents.

Next, I leveraged my network and reached out to more experienced colleagues for advice. Their insights were invaluable, and their encouragement boosted my confidence. I also made a point of staying positive, even when faced with setbacks. There were times when showings didn't go as planned, or offers fell through, but I remained focused on my goal and kept a positive outlook.

One particular incident stands out. During an open house, I noticed that a potential buyer seemed very interested but hesitant. Instead of pushing for an immediate decision, I took the time to listen to their concerns and answer all their questions patiently. My confidence in the property's value and my positive, reassuring demeanor helped put them at ease. They later returned with an offer that exceeded our expectations.

Ultimately, the property sold for a record price in the neighborhood, and the client was thrilled. This success was a turning point for me. It reinforced the importance of confidence and positivity in achieving professional success. By believing in myself and maintaining an optimistic outlook, I was able to overcome challenges and exceed expectations. Confidence and positivity are not innate traits but skills that can be developed with practice and perseverance.

Courage is an entrepreneur's secret weapon, serving as the inner fire that propels you forward in the face of challenges. It's the reassuring voice that whispers, "You've got this," whenever doubt begins to creep in. However, confidence is not synonymous with perfection or the absence of uncertainty. Instead, it revolves around the belief in your ability to learn, grow, and overcome obstacles. This belief is crucial for success and strengthens with practice - much like a muscle, the more you exercise your confidence, the stronger it becomes.

I've always admired Oprah Winfrey for her remarkable confidence and positive thinking. Born into poverty in rural Mississippi and facing abuse and discrimination, Oprah refused to let these hardships define her. Her natural talent for communication and unwavering self-belief propelled her into the media industry. At 19, she became the youngest African American female news anchor at Nashville's WLAC-TV.[11]

Oprah's authentic approach to broadcasting, marked by emotional openness and personal stories, became the foundation of her success with "The Oprah Winfrey Show" in 1986. She maintained a positive outlook despite setbacks and criticism, embodying her belief that "You become what you believe."

Her confidence extended to her challenges, including struggles with weight and self-image, which she turned into opportunities to inspire others. Oprah's willingness to take risks, such as launching her network, OWN, in 2011, despite initial difficulties, highlights her belief in overcoming obstacles.

Positivity complements confidence; it embodies the ability to maintain an optimistic outlook, even in adversity. It involves focusing on solutions rather than dwelling on

11   Andrew Bloomenthal, "Oprah Winfrey: Early Life and Education, Notable Accomplishments, and Philanthropy," Investopedia, updated January 10, 2024, accessed July 30, 2024, https://www.investopedia.com/articles/insights/072816/how-did-oprah-winfrey-get-rich.asp.

problems and believing that setbacks are temporary and surmountable. Together, confidence and positivity form a powerful combination that can propel entrepreneurs to new heights, enabling them to handle the unpredictable waters of entrepreneurship.

The foundation of confidence lies in self-awareness. Understanding your strengths and weaknesses equips you to set realistic goals and develop actionable strategies to achieve them. Additionally, authenticity plays a significant role in fostering confidence. By being true to yourself, you build trust and credibility with others, which is essential in establishing meaningful connections within your industry.

Moreover, maintaining a positive attitude can significantly improve mental resilience, enhance problem-solving skills, and cultivate a supportive and productive environment. When challenges arise, those with a positive mindset are more likely to view them as opportunities for growth rather than insurmountable obstacles.

Ultimately, confidence and positivity together create a mindset that empowers individuals to take bold actions, persist through difficulties, and inspire others to do the same. They are not merely traits; they are skills that can be cultivated and strengthened over time. These qualities are contagious. A confident and positive entrepreneur can inspire their team, attract investors, and win over customers. Their enthusiasm and belief in their vision can be the differentiating factor in a competitive market.

By consciously developing these qualities, entrepreneurs can unlock their potential and move through their journeys with greater assurance and optimism, leading to sustained success and fulfillment in their endeavors.

LESSONS IN CONFIDENCE AND OPTIMISM

Through my experiences, I learned several valuable lessons that have shaped my approach to challenges in my career. First and foremost, I discovered the importance of resilience. The skepticism I faced early on was disheartening, but it ignited a fire within me to prove that my circumstances would not define my capabilities. I realized that resilience is not just about bouncing back from difficulties; it's about embracing challenges as opportunities for growth. I understood that the obstacles I encountered could be powerful motivators, propelling me to push my boundaries and develop the skills needed to overcome adversity. This shift in perspective allowed me to approach my career with a newfound determination and strength.

Preparation emerged as another critical lesson in my journey. I understood that thorough research and a comprehensive understanding of the market were paramount to building confidence. Investing time in learning about property values, local trends, and competitive analysis equipped me with the knowledge needed to handle complex situations. By presenting myself as knowledgeable and credible, I instilled confidence not only in myself but also in my clients and colleagues. This preparation proved invaluable, enabling me to succeed in selling properties and laying a strong foundation for my future endeavors. It taught me that preparation is a crucial investment that pays dividends in self-assurance and success.

Seeking support and guidance from experienced colleagues was invaluable. Their insights and encouragement reminded me that I was not alone in my journey. Building a network of mentors and peers provided a safety net that boosted my confidence and offered diverse perspectives on navigating challenges. This network became a source of inspiration and practical advice, reminding me that asking for help is not a sign of weakness; rather, it demonstrates a commitment to growth and a willingness to learn from others. Collaborating with those who have faced similar challenges allowed me to glean valuable lessons that would have taken me much longer to learn on my own.

Additionally, I recognized the power of positivity. Maintaining an optimistic outlook in the face of setbacks allowed me to stay focused on my goals. This positive mindset became my anchor, teaching me that the way I approached challenges could significantly influence the outcomes. Rather than viewing setbacks as failures, I began to see them as opportunities to refine my approach and improve my strategies. A positive attitude not only opened doors to new opportunities but also helped create an environment where collaboration and innovation flourished among my peers and team members.

Finally, I learned that confidence is not an innate trait but a skill that can be developed over time. Every challenge I overcame reinforced my self-belief and encouraged me to continue pushing beyond my limits. Each success, no matter how small, contributed to a growing sense of confidence that empowered me to take on new challenges with greater ease. This journey solidified my understanding that success is not solely measured by achievements but also by the strength of character cultivated along the way. The lessons I learned in confidence and optimism taught me that embracing the journey, with all its ups and downs, is essential for personal and professional growth.

Confidence and optimism are not merely traits but essential components of a successful career. By embracing resilience, preparing thoroughly, seeking support, maintaining a positive outlook, and recognizing that confidence can be cultivated, I have equipped myself with the tools to face any challenge head-on.

HOW TO BUILD YOUR CONFIDENCE

1. Practice Self-Affirmation

Self-affirmation is an incredibly powerful tool for building confidence, especially in the entrepreneurial world. By starting each day with positive affirmations, you set a tone of self-belief and resilience that can carry you through the challenges ahead. Begin each morning by looking in the mirror and saying, "I am capable, I am resilient, and I have the strength to overcome any business challenge." These affirmations are not just words; they are reminders of your inherent strength and capability.

Regularly remind yourself of your strengths, achievements, and potential. Think back to the significant obstacles you've already overcome, such as leaving a steady job to pursue your entrepreneurial dreams, learning new skills, or securing your first investor. Write down your strengths and past successes, and read them whenever you're feeling doubtful. This practice reinforces the belief that you have what it takes to succeed, grounding your confidence in real, tangible experiences. Your entrepreneurial journey itself is a testament to your capabilities.

2. Prepare Thoroughly

Preparation is a cornerstone of confidence, particularly in business. When you're well-prepared, you equip yourself with the knowledge and readiness to tackle challenges head-on, which naturally boosts your confidence. This is especially true when you're entering new markets or pitching to investors. The more you know, the more confident you'll feel in these high-stakes situations. For instance, if you have an important meeting, research the attendees and their companies thoroughly.

If you're attending an industry conference, learn about the key trends and topics that will be discussed. Being informed not only boosts your confidence but also enables you to engage more effectively in discussions, ask insightful questions, and leave a strong impression. Before key events, consider adopting a confident posture, such as standing tall with your hands on your hips for two minutes. This technique, often referred to as a "power pose," was popularized by research from Amy Cuddy[12] Although subsequent research has yielded mixed results, many people report feeling more confident after adopting such postures. This straightforward technique could positively influence your mindset and potentially your performance. Ultimately, preparation combined with these confidence-boosting techniques will help you face any business challenge with assurance.

3. Embrace Self-Care

Self-care is more than just a wellness trend; it's a critical aspect of maintaining the confidence needed to navigate the demands of entrepreneurship. Taking care of your physical and mental health contributes significantly to your overall confidence. When you feel good physically and mentally, you're more likely to approach business challenges with a positive and resilient mindset. Running a business can be stressful, and it's easy to neglect self-care. However, maintaining your health is crucial for building resilience and confidence as an entrepreneur.

Establish a routine that prioritizes your well-being, including

---

12   Julia Hanna, "Power Posing: Fake It Until You Make It," **Business Research for Business Leaders**, Harvard Business Reviews, September 20, 2010, https://hbswk.hbs.edu/item/power-posing-fake-it-until-you-make-it.

regular exercise, a balanced diet, and adequate sleep. Find ways to manage stress that work for you - it could be meditation, yoga, or a hobby you enjoy. These activities not only help you unwind but also recharge your mental and emotional energy, making you more effective in your business endeavors. Don't forget about mental health - if you're struggling, seek support from professionals or peer groups for entrepreneurs. Recognizing when you need help and taking steps to get it is a sign of strength, not weakness, and it plays a vital role in sustaining your confidence over the long term.

4. Visualize Success

Visualization is a powerful mental technique that can significantly enhance your confidence as an entrepreneur. By regularly imagining yourself succeeding in your business endeavors, you reinforce a positive mindset and build the psychological foundation for real-world success. Visualize yourself delivering a perfect pitch, closing a big deal, or seeing your product change people's lives. This practice of mental rehearsal can be especially beneficial before facing challenging situations.

For example, if you're nervous about a presentation to investors, close your eyes and imagine yourself delivering it confidently and receiving positive feedback. This visualization exercise helps reduce anxiety, aligns your mental state with success, and can significantly boost your actual performance when the time comes. The more vividly you can imagine these positive outcomes, the more likely you are to approach your business challenges with the confidence that success is within reach. Over time, this practice not only boosts your confidence but also conditions your mind to expect and achieve success.

5. Learn from Failures

Failure is an inevitable part of the entrepreneurial journey, but it's how you respond to setbacks that define your path to success. Learning from failures rather than dwelling on them is key to building lasting confidence. Setbacks are inevitable in business. The key is to reframe these experiences as valuable learning opportunities rather than personal deficiencies. For instance, if a product launch doesn't go as planned, don't berate yourself - instead, see it as a chance to gather valuable market feedback.

This shift in perspective allows you to maintain your confidence even in the face of adversity. Every successful entrepreneur has faced failures along the way. What sets them apart is their ability to learn and grow from these experiences. To help with this, keep a "lessons learned" journal where you document what happened after each setback and, more importantly, what you learned from it. Over time, you'll see how these experiences have contributed to your growth and resilience as an entrepreneur. This journal not only helps you track your progress but also serves as a reminder of your ability to overcome obstacles and emerge stronger, reinforcing your confidence with each new challenge you face.

Confidence and positivity are crucial for achieving success in any field. By cultivating a confident mindset and sustaining a positive outlook, you can effectively manage challenges, embrace risks, and reach your goals. These qualities are not innate; they can be developed over time through practice and perseverance. Embrace the journey of growth and self-improvement, and you'll discover that confidence and positivity become powerful allies in your pursuit of success.

REFLECT AND ACT

1. What three positive affirmations about your abilities as an entrepreneur can you write and recite daily?

2. How does practicing a "power pose" before important events affect your confidence levels? What changes do you notice?

3. What small accomplishment or victory, no matter how minor, can you acknowledge in yourself today?

4. How can you develop a daily routine that reinforces positive self-belief?

5. What strategies can you use to boost your confidence before high-stakes situations?

6. How do you plan to celebrate your daily achievements, both big and small?

7. What role does self-affirmation play in maintaining your overall entrepreneurial mindset?

Principle #9

TURN DISADVANTAGES INTO STRATEGIC ADVANTAGES

"In the middle of difficulty lies opportunity."

- ALBERT EINSTEIN

Taking what others might see as your weaknesses and turning them into your greatest strengths is a powerful secret that can transform your entrepreneurial journey. When you cultivate this shift in mindset, you unlock doors you never thought possible, propelling yourself toward success in ways you may not have imagined. This principle is about recognizing the value in your unique experiences and traits, using them creatively to overcome challenges and stand out in the marketplace.

When I faced what many would consider a significant disadvantage – being pregnant, I could have just thrown in the towel. The lady's words could have been discouraging, but I chose to see them as a challenge. Her skeptical "Well, we'll see" only propelled me to success.

Connecting this experience to my broader entrepreneurial journey, I realized that my perceived disadvantage could be turned into a unique story of resilience and success. This was not the first time I had faced skepticism, and it certainly wouldn't be the last. Each time, I chose to see these challenges as opportunities to prove my worth and capability.

One particularly memorable moment was when I was told I was at a disadvantage because of my race. A mentor advised against using my photo on business cards, suggesting it would hinder my prospects due to my skin color. As an immigrant, this perspective was new to me, but I refused to conform to the bias. I proudly used those business cards and continued to secure business through persistence and dedication.

Another perceived disadvantage I faced was my accent. Some questioned my ability based solely on how I spoke the English language. In response, I calmly reminded them that accents are a common aspect of communication diversity. I emphasized that mutual understanding and effective communication matter more than where someone comes from or how they speak. I did not allow my accent to change my value. Instead, I focused on bringing exceptional value to every interaction and opportunity. As a result, my accent became desirable - a mark of my international experience and diverse perspective. People began to see it as an asset rather than a limitation. It became a symbol of the unique insights and global understanding I brought to the table. It set me apart in a positive way, adding depth to my professional identity.

By embracing my unique traits and using them to my advantage, I was able to differentiate myself in the market and build a successful career.

Limited resources can ignite innovation and creativity, pushing you to think outside the box and develop novel solutions. A lack of experience can become an asset, granting you a fresh perspective unencumbered by conventional wisdom. External biases may present challenges, but they can also fuel your determination and resilience, motivating you to prove naysayers wrong and achieve your goals.

Furthermore, your unique background and experiences allow you to connect with a diverse array of people and perspectives. This diversity is a powerful tool for identifying unmet needs, creating innovative products or services, and building a loyal customer base.

Many successful entrepreneurs have thrived by reinterpreting challenges such as limited resources, lack of experience, and external biases as opportunities for growth. For instance, a scarcity of resources can compel you to discover cost-effective solutions, ultimately fostering greater efficiency. Shahid Khan,13 transformed his outsider perspective into a billion-dollar auto parts empire, while Satya Nadella's leadership at Microsoft14 exemplifies how to manage limited

---

13   "Flex-N-Gate Overview." Zippia. Accessed July 1, 2024. https://www.zippia.com/flex-n-gate-careers-23580/.

14   Naomi Buchanan, "Microsoft CEO Nadella Says He's 'Optimistic'

resources effectively and create value, even when starting from a position of financial constraints.

Rather than simply cutting costs or maximizing short-term profits, Nadella has consistently emphasized creating value for customers. This approach has led to significant innovations and growth, even in areas where Microsoft was not traditionally strong. His tenure has also been characterized by strategic resource allocation, with the company making significant investments in cloud computing and artificial intelligence - areas that have driven substantial growth. This demonstrates the importance of allocating limited resources to high-potential areas rather than spreading them too thin.

Your entrepreneurial journey has equipped you with a wealth of experiences and insights that are uniquely yours. By embracing and strategically leveraging these assets, you can create a distinctive advantage in your field, transforming potential obstacles into stepping stones toward success. As the ancient philosopher Epictetus wisely noted, "It's not what happens to you, but how you react to it that matters."15 Your true power lies not in the circumstances you encounter, but in how you perceive and harness them. By reframing

---

About AI's Future and Global Standards," Investopedia, published January 16, 2024, accessed July 31, 2024, https://www.investopedia.com/microsoft-ceo-satya-nadella-says-he-is-optimistic-about-the-future-of-ai-and-global-standards-8426736.

15   Epictetus. "It's not what happens to you, but how you react to it that matters." Commonly attributed quote.

your perceived disadvantages as unique strengths, you open yourself to a world of possibilities.

THE STRENGTH IN YOUR IDENTITY

Challenges, often perceived as obstacles, can become powerful catalysts for growth when approached with resilience and determination. Each setback presents a unique opportunity to reflect on one's strengths and capabilities. Skepticism and bias should not deter your progress; instead, they can fuel your drive to prove yourself and achieve success. Rather than seeing doubt from others as a barrier, I learned to view it as motivation to excel and demonstrate the value of my contributions. This mindset shift transformed adversity into an avenue for empowerment.

One of the most important lessons I learned is the necessity of standing firm against discrimination and using your identity as a source of strength. Facing bias head-on can be daunting, but it is essential to maintain confidence in your abilities. When confronted with prejudice, I found that acknowledging my unique perspective and experiences provided me with a solid foundation to build upon. This commitment to self-acceptance fosters resilience and the belief that your worth is not determined by others' opinions. It's crucial to recognize that while discrimination may be a reality, your identity is not defined by these negative experiences; instead, it can be a source of empowerment that drives you forward.

Moreover, I discovered the significance of communication

diversity in overcoming biases. Effective communication and mutual understanding are not limited by accents or linguistic differences. I learned that what matters most is the message you convey and the sincerity behind it. By focusing on the value you bring to interactions, you can turn perceived disadvantages, such as an accent, into unique assets. This perspective highlights the richness of diverse backgrounds and the depth they contribute to both professional and personal identities. Embracing communication diversity allows for more inclusive environments where ideas can flourish. Rather than shying away from differences, I found that celebrating them fosters stronger connections and enhances collaboration.

My experiences underscored the power of embracing and leveraging your unique traits. In moments of doubt, I discovered that my distinct background and experiences could be transformed into powerful narratives that resonate with others. Challenges should be viewed as opportunities to showcase resilience, adaptability, and ingenuity. For instance, I learned to share my story in a way that highlights the strength I derived from overcoming obstacles, effectively transforming my narrative from one of struggle to one of triumph. This shift not only reinforced my sense of self but also inspired others who faced similar challenges.

Furthermore, I realized the importance of cultivating a strong support network. Connecting with individuals who share your experiences or can relate to your journey can be incredibly empowering. Mentorship played a pivotal role in my development, as I sought out mentors who embraced their identities and faced adversity head-on. Their guidance and support provided me with invaluable insights and encouragement. This community became a source of strength, reinforcing the idea that I am not alone in my journey. The relationships I built helped me overcome challenges and fostered a sense of belonging that fueled my ambitions.

As I continued to grow in my career, I also recognized the importance of advocating for yourself and others. By standing up against biases and discrimination, you can contribute to creating a more inclusive environment for everyone. I learned that using my voice to champion diversity not only benefits me but also empowers others to embrace their identities. This collective effort strengthens our communities and fosters a culture of acceptance and understanding.

Finally, I came to understand that true strength lies in authenticity. Embracing your identity fully and unapologetically allows you to bring your genuine self to every interaction. This authenticity is not just a personal strength but a professional asset that sets you apart in a competitive landscape. When you are true to yourself, you attract opportunities that align with your values and vision. This alignment is essential for sustained success and fulfillment, reinforcing the idea that your unique identity is a powerful tool for growth.

In conclusion, challenges and biases can serve as catalysts for personal and professional growth when approached with resilience and determination. By standing firm in your identity, embracing communication diversity, leveraging unique traits, and building a supportive network, you can turn obstacles into stepping stones toward success. Ultimately, the strength in your identity not only propels your journey but also inspires others to embrace their paths, fostering a culture of inclusivity and empowerment.

HOW TO TURN PERCEIVED DISADVANTAGES INTO STRATEGIC ADVANTAGES

1. Identify and Reframe Your Unique Traits

Start by making a comprehensive list of what you or others might see as your disadvantages. This could include your non-traditional career path, lack of industry-specific experience, or any perceived gaps in your knowledge. Once you have this list, challenge yourself to reframe each item positively. For example:

- *Lack of industry-specific experience:* It means you bring fresh perspectives and innovative ideas unconstrained by "how things have always been done."

- *Non-traditional career path:* It shows your adaptability, diverse skill set, and ability to succeed in various contexts.

This exercise isn't just about positive thinking - it's about recognizing the genuine value in your unique experiences and traits. Keep this list handy and refer to it often, especially when you're feeling doubtful or facing challenges. Take it a step further by crafting a personal brand statement that incorporates these reframed traits. For example: "I am an innovative entrepreneur with diverse experience, bringing fresh ideas to drive business growth." Use this statement as a foundation for your business pitch, website, and networking conversations. By consistently presenting your unique traits as valuable assets, you'll not only convince others of your worth but also reinforce your self-belief.

2. Seek Opportunities Where Your Background is an Asset

Now that you've reframed your unique traits positively, it's time to seek out opportunities where these traits are particularly valuable. This strategy is about aligning your distinctive background with markets and industries where it can shine. Start by researching industries and market segments that could benefit from your unique perspective. Look for:

- Markets where your particular insights could provide a competitive edge
- Industries experiencing disruption where fresh perspectives are valued
- Niches where your diverse experiences could lead to innovative solutions

Don't limit yourself to traditional business models. Attend

industry events, join professional associations, and participate in diverse networking groups. These can be goldmines for finding opportunities where your background is seen as an asset rather than a liability. Consider how your unique perspective might allow you to spot gaps in the market that others have missed - many successful businesses have been built by entrepreneurs who use their cross-industry or cross-cultural insights to create innovative products or services.

When pitching to investors or clients, tailor your presentation to highlight how your unique background makes you especially suited to solve the problem you're addressing. For example, if your business aims to revolutionize an industry you're new to, emphasize how your outsider perspective allows you to see opportunities for innovation that industry veterans might miss. Remember, you're not just looking for any business idea - you're looking for opportunities where your perceived disadvantages can become your greatest strengths. Be patient and persistent in this search. The right opportunity might take time to find, but when you do, you'll be in a position to truly excel.

3. Develop Complementary Skills and Share Your Story

While your unique background is a significant asset, it's important to complement it with skills that enhance your overall package as an entrepreneur. This is about creating a combination of your distinctive traits and widely valued business skills. Start by identifying skills that are highly valued in entrepreneurship. These might include:

- Financial management and budgeting
- Marketing and sales
- Project management
- Leadership and team management
- Data analysis and interpretation

Invest time in developing these skills through online courses, workshops, or by taking on projects that allow you to practice them. The goal is to create a unique skill set that combines your distinctive background with broadly applicable business abilities. For example, if you're starting a tech company, you might combine your innovative product ideas with strong financial modeling skills. This allows you to not only create cutting-edge products but also present a compelling business case to investors - a powerful combination. Equally important is learning to share your entrepreneurial story effectively.

Your journey is rich with experiences that demonstrate resilience, adaptability, and problem-solving skills. Learning to articulate this story can set you apart in investor meetings, networking events, and client pitches. Develop a few key stories that illustrate how your background has prepared you for entrepreneurial success. Practice telling these stories - focus on the challenges you've overcome and the unique perspectives you've gained. Remember, it's not just about what you've done but what you've learned and how it applies to your business goals. Consider starting a blog or being active on professional social media platforms to share your insights. This can establish you as a thought leader at the intersection of your unique background and your industry.

By developing complementary skills and learning to share your story effectively, you create a unique entrepreneurial profile that's hard to ignore. You're not just another startup founder - you're someone with a distinctive combination of skills, experiences, and insights that can add unique value to the market.

4. Practice Self-Affirmation

Self-affirmation is a powerful tool in building confidence. Start each morning by looking in the mirror and saying, "I am capable, I am resilient, and I have the strength to overcome any business challenge." Regularly remind yourself of your strengths, achievements, and potential. Remember the perceived disadvantages you've already overcome - perhaps leaving a steady job, learning new skills, or securing your first investor. These are significant achievements. Write down your strengths and past successes. Read them when you're feeling doubtful. Your entrepreneurial journey itself is a testament to your capabilities.

5. Visualize Success

Regularly imagine yourself succeeding in your business

endeavors to reinforce a positive mindset. Visualize yourself delivering a perfect pitch, closing a big deal, or seeing your product change people's lives. This technique can be particularly helpful before challenging situations. If you're nervous about a presentation to investors, close your eyes and imagine yourself delivering it confidently and receiving positive feedback. This mental rehearsal can significantly boost your actual performance.

Turning perceived disadvantages into advantages is a powerful principle that can transform your entrepreneurial journey. Embrace your unique circumstances and use them to set yourself apart. Every perceived disadvantage is an opportunity in disguise - one that can fuel your creativity, drive innovation, and differentiate you from the competition. By reframing obstacles as opportunities, you cultivate resilience and adaptability, both of which are essential traits for entrepreneurial success.

Your ability to turn perceived disadvantages into advantages will not only define your success but also inspire others along the way. When you leverage your unique experiences and traits, you demonstrate that success is achievable despite any obstacles. This mindset encourages others to view their challenges as potential strengths. In doing so, you foster a culture of empowerment and innovation, proving that true success lies in harnessing the power of your unique journey.

Embrace your distinctiveness, and watch how it propels you to new heights.

REFLECT AND ACT

1. What traits or experiences do you currently see as disadvantages? How could each of these potentially be an asset in your career or personal life?

2. What unique insights or skills do you possess? How could each of these be valuable in your business?

3. What specific opportunities or niches in your market could benefit from your unconventional background or perspective?

4. How can you leverage your unique background to differentiate yourself from competitors?

5. What past experiences have equipped you with skills that are underutilized in your current role?

6. How can you turn perceived weaknesses into strengths that benefit your business?

7. What steps can you take to position your unique perspective as an advantage in your industry?

Principle #10

STRIVE FOR EXCELLENCE TO BECOME THE BEST VERSION OF YOURSELF

"To give anything less than your best is to sacrifice the gift."

- STEVE PREFONTAINE

Excellence is about consistently putting forth your best effort, learning from every experience, and striving for improvement - not perfection. In the competitive world of business, excellence opens doors, builds relationships, and paves the way for your desired success.

Consider excellence as your brand. In a marketplace where you may initially be seen as "just another startup," your commitment to quality and willingness to go above and beyond will set you apart. Excellence transcends industries; it is a universal language that helps you bridge gaps, earn respect, and create opportunities.

From the moment I decided to enter the real estate industry, I knew mediocrity was not an option. My journey has been marked by a relentless pursuit of excellence and a determination to make a significant impact. This drive led me to remarkable success, ranking among the top 50 agents nationwide and becoming Delaware's number-one agent.

In just a few years, I transformed from a newcomer to a legend in the real estate industry. My first two years were marked by record-breaking sales, and I earned titles such as Top Dollar Agent, Top Real Estate Agent, and Rising Star Agent. In 2022, I joined eXp Realty, a Fortune 500 company with over 94,000 agents globally. I set a bold goal of 100 sales - and I achieved it!

The relentless pursuit of excellence isn't unique to any single field. It's a universal principle that drives success across various domains. Chimamanda Ngozi Adichie's journey profoundly exemplifies this principle. Despite facing challenging circumstances in Nigeria, Adichie's unwavering commitment to her craft was evident in her breakthrough novel, "Half of a Yellow Sun." Her dedication to her writing, even amidst adversity, highlights her pursuit of excellence. This is reflected in traditional Igbo wisdom: 'When the moon is shining, the cripple becomes hungry for a walk.' This saying captures the essence of relentless ambition, illustrating that even in the face of significant obstacles, the drive to achieve greatness remains a powerful and unyielding force.

Success in the real estate market requires a deep understanding of market dynamics, unwavering commitment to clients, and dedication to continuous learning and improvement. To stand out, I honed my skills, stayed updated with industry trends, and provided exceptional service to every client.

There were temptations to cut corners for quick gains. For instance, I once had the opportunity to withhold information about upcoming construction that might affect a property's value. Instead, I chose to disclose this information to potential buyers, even though it made the sale more challenging. This commitment to ethical excellence sometimes cost me in the short term but built a reputation for integrity that became one of my greatest assets in the long run.

Even as I achieved success, I never stopped looking for ways to improve. I was among the first in my market to embrace digital marketing strategies, use data analytics for pricing strategies, and implement a Customer Relationship Management (CRM) system to better serve my clients. This commitment to innovation helped me stay ahead of market trends and maintain my position as an industry leader.

My dedication paid off. I began to attract high-profile clients and successfully closed several high-value transactions - 300 homes, generating more than $80 million in sales within four years.

My reputation for excellence in the market grew, and I started receiving referrals from satisfied clients. This success was not just about the financial rewards; it was about the trust and confidence my clients placed in me. They knew that I would go above and beyond to meet their needs and exceed their expectations.

The higher I climbed, the more I understood the importance of maintaining unwavering excellence. Transparency, meticulous attention to detail, and an unyielding commitment to doing things right became non-negotiable principles guiding my professional conduct.

When you consistently deliver outstanding work, you build a reputation that precedes you, establishing trust and credibility with clients, partners, and stakeholders. People are more likely to engage with you and support your endeavors when they recognize your dedication to excellence. This commitment demonstrates that you value your work and are focused on achieving the best possible outcomes.

Excellence embodies resilience and adaptability. In a constantly changing business environment, learning from experiences and striving to improve is invaluable. Embracing feedback, learning from mistakes, and seeking new knowledge ensures you remain competitive, regardless of market evolution.

Moreover, excellence fosters innovation. By pushing the boundaries of what is possible, you encourage the exploration of new ideas, calculated risks, and creative solutions to complex problems. Your pursuit of excellence enhances your capabilities and inspires those around you to aim higher.

Becoming the number-one agent in Delaware and gaining national recognition was the culmination of years of hard work, perseverance, and a commitment to excellence. It was a journey filled with challenges and setbacks, but each obstacle only strengthened my resolve. I learned to view challenges as opportunities for growth and improvement. Instead of being discouraged by setbacks, I used them as motivation to push harder and aim higher.

Building on my initial national recognition, my continued excellence in the field has garnered even more attention. My story has been featured in prominent industry publications, and I've been invited to speak at various conferences and seminars. This ongoing exposure has opened up new opportunities, including partnerships and collaborations with other top professionals in the industry. It has also given me the platform to share my knowledge and experience with aspiring real estate agents, helping them achieve their success.

LESSONS IN ACHIEVING A LEGENDARY STATUS

These experiences have underscored that excellence is not a final destination but an ongoing journey. It embodies a commitment to continuous improvement, learning, and adaptation. Achieving a legendary status is about setting high standards in every facet of your business and persistently striving to surpass them. In real estate, as in any industry, this unwavering commitment to excellence can serve as your key differentiator and the bedrock of a legendary success.

The lessons I've learned and the benchmarks of excellence I've established in my real estate career have formed the cornerstone of my achievements, continually propelling me forward.

Striving for excellence means never settling for mediocrity; it involves a relentless pursuit of improvement, innovation, and quality. This pursuit permeates every aspect of the business, shaping how you present yourself and how you serve your clients. Whether it's in the meticulous preparation of a property listing, the personalized service provided to clients, or the strategic approach to market trends, maintaining a high standard ensures that every aspect of the business reflects a commitment to superior performance. This dedication not only enhances the client experience but also elevates your professional reputation, positioning you as a leader in the field.

Moreover, excellence requires a proactive mindset. It's about anticipating client needs, staying ahead of industry changes, and continuously educating oneself to remain at the forefront of the field. This proactive approach includes embracing new technologies, understanding emerging market trends, and seeking opportunities for professional development. By committing to lifelong learning, you can identify potential challenges before they arise, allowing you to adapt your strategies accordingly. This adaptability enhances your reputation and builds trust and loyalty among clients and colleagues, as they recognize your commitment to staying informed and delivering exceptional service.

Excellence also fosters a culture of accountability and integrity. When you hold yourself to the highest standards, you set a precedent for those around you. This expectation creates an environment where everyone is motivated to perform at their best. Cultivating a culture of excellence encourages team members to take ownership of their responsibilities and to strive for continuous improvement. As each individual works toward their highest potential, the collective pursuit of excellence drives the entire team toward greater achievements and sustained success.

Additionally, the pursuit of excellence often requires embracing feedback and constructive criticism. Being open to feedback from clients, peers, and mentors can lead to invaluable insights that drive your growth. Rather than viewing criticism as a setback, consider it an opportunity to refine your approach and enhance your offerings. This willingness to learn from others not only strengthens your skills but also fosters a collaborative spirit within your team, promoting an environment where everyone feels valued and empowered to contribute to the collective success.

Furthermore, excellence is rooted in authenticity. Staying true to your values and mission allows you to connect more deeply with your clients and community. This genuine approach fosters trust and builds long-lasting relationships, enhancing your reputation as a reliable and principled professional. By aligning your actions with your core beliefs, you create a brand that resonates with clients and inspires loyalty, further solidifying your status in the industry.

In conclusion, achieving a legendary status requires an ongoing commitment to excellence that permeates every aspect of your professional journey. By continuously striving for improvement, adopting a proactive mindset, fostering a culture of accountability, embracing feedback, and staying true to your authentic self, you can pave the way for not only your success but also the success of those around you. These lessons serve as a foundation for building a legacy of excellence that inspires others to pursue their aspirations and achieve their renowned status.

HOW TO CULTIVATE EXCELLENCE

1. Set High Standards for Yourself

Cultivating excellence begins with setting high standards for yourself. This involves consistently striving to deliver your best work, no matter the task at hand. Whether you're cleaning your workspace, drafting an email, or working on a major project, approaching each task with thoroughness and precision is crucial. Excellence is not about perfection but about consistently aiming to improve and grow. Setting clear goals is an essential part of this process. Define both short-term and long-term objectives, writing them down and breaking them into actionable steps.

Regularly reviewing and adjusting these goals will help you maintain high standards and stay on track toward your ambitions. Patience is also key; excellence is a continuous journey of learning and self-improvement. As you strive for high standards, you'll develop habits that will permeate all aspects of your professional and personal life, driving you toward sustained success.

2. Never Stop Learning

In a rapidly changing world, the pursuit of knowledge is vital for those who aspire to excellence. Continuous learning keeps you sharp and adaptable, enabling you to stay ahead of industry trends and innovations. Make it a habit to read books, attend workshops, take online courses, and watch educational videos regularly. This commitment to lifelong learning will not only expand your knowledge base but also open up new opportunities for growth and improvement.

Don't be afraid to ask questions or seek clarification when you encounter something unfamiliar in your business. Surround yourself with mentors who have succeeded in your field; their insights and experiences can be invaluable, helping you avoid common pitfalls and accelerate your progress. Embracing a mindset of continuous education ensures that you remain relevant and competitive in your industry, positioning you for long-term success.

3. Pay Attention to Details

Attention to detail is a distinguishing characteristic of those who excel. The small things often make a significant difference, whether it's catching errors before they become costly mistakes or adding the finishing touches that elevate a project from good to great. Being meticulous requires a disciplined approach to your work. Double-checking your work, whether it's a simple email or a complex report, ensures accuracy and quality. Staying organized is also crucial for managing details effectively.

Keep your workspace tidy, use calendars and to-do lists to track tasks and deadlines, and utilize apps or tools that help you stay on top of your responsibilities. This organization not only helps you manage your workload more efficiently but also allows you to focus on the quality of your work. Over time, a reputation for reliability and high-quality output will set you apart from others and establish you as a leader in your field.

4. Ask for Feedback

Excellence is a continuous process of refinement, and one of the most effective ways to refine your skills is by seeking feedback. While asking for feedback can be intimidating, especially when it involves constructive criticism, it is an invaluable tool for growth. Actively seek input from colleagues, mentors, or even clients, and approach their suggestions with an open mind. Avoid becoming defensive; instead, view feedback as an opportunity to improve and excel.

Networking plays a significant role in this process as well. By building strong professional relationships through industry events, professional organizations, or volunteer work, you can gain access to diverse perspectives and valuable advice. When

I sought feedback from industry leaders, their insights not only helped me refine my skills but also provided guidance that shaped my career trajectory. Embracing feedback as a tool for continuous improvement will enhance your expertise and propel you toward greater achievements.

5. Go the Extra Mile

True excellence involves consistently going beyond what is expected. When you complete a task or project, think about additional ways to add value. This could mean conducting extra research, offering additional insights, or taking the initiative to improve processes. Going the extra mile also extends beyond your professional life. Consider how you can contribute to your community, whether through formal volunteer work, mentoring others, or simply being a supportive friend or neighbor.

These actions not only build your reputation for excellence but also create positive ripple effects in your personal and professional networks. Over time, this habit of exceeding expectations will open new opportunities and foster strong relationships. By continually striving to do more and provide additional value, you not only demonstrate your commitment to excellence but also inspire others to raise their standards, creating a culture of excellence around you.

Excellence cultivates a culture of high performance within your organization. By leading by example, you set a standard for others to follow, fostering a motivated workforce where team members take pride in their work and strive for their best.

Embracing excellence in all that you do will elevate your journey and inspire those around you to aim higher. Commit to being the best version of yourself, and witness how it transforms both your personal and professional life.

Excellence is a lifelong journey of continuous improvement. Some days will be more challenging than others, but persistence is key. Your unwavering commitment to excellence will not only drive your success but also inspire your team, partners, and clients. Believe in yourself, remain dedicated to your goals, and never stop striving to be your best.

Keep progressing, keep evolving, and keep shining! By consistently aiming high, staying curious, paying attention to details, seeking feedback, and going the extra mile, you can build a foundation of excellence that establishes you as a legend in your field.

REFLECT AND ACT

1. What are three high standards you want to set for yourself in your business? How will you measure your progress towards them?

2. In what area of your business can you "go the extra mile" this week? What specific actions will you take?

3. How can you celebrate your achievements more effectively? What system can you put in place to regularly acknowledge your progress?

4. How do you plan to maintain high standards without compromising on work-life balance?

5. What metrics will you use to track the impact of going the extra mile in your business?

6. How can you create a culture of excellence within your team or organization?

7. What role does celebrating achievements play in sustaining long-term motivation and success?

CONCLUSION

As we close the final chapter of "From Ordinary to Extraordinary," I want you to pause and reflect on the incredible journey that lies ahead of you. This book isn't just a collection of principles; it's a blueprint for transforming your entrepreneurial vision into reality and leaving an indelible mark on the world.

Your unique journey, with all its twists and turns, has forged within you a power unlike any other. The challenges you've faced, the resilience you've developed, and the fresh ideas you bring are the very ingredients that will fuel your rise to a legendary status. Embrace them fully, for they are your greatest assets in a world crying out for authentic, transformative leaders. Remember, success isn't about never falling; it's about rising every time we fall. Like my experience of failing the real estate exam three times, your setbacks are stepping stones to greatness. Cultivate belief in yourself through consistent action and small victories. Even if doubt creeps in, take small steps, celebrate progress, and surround yourself with supportive people.

The principles we've explored are more than mere concepts — they're the battle-tested tools that have launched empires and reshaped industries. But knowledge without action is like a seed never planted. Your task now is to breathe life into what you've learned, to water it with your sweat, and to nurture it with unwavering commitment.

Imagine your future self, standing atop the mountain of your achievements. What does that version of you look like? What impact have you made? Let this vision burn bright in your mind's eye, becoming the North Star that guides you through the storms of doubt and the fog of uncertainty.

Embrace change not as a threat, but as your greatest ally. In a world of constant change, your ability to adapt and innovate is your competitive edge. When others see obstacles, train your mind to see opportunities. Where tradition says "impossible," let your entrepreneurial spirit whisper "Let's revolutionize."

Cultivate your mindset with the same fervor an athlete trains their body. Feed your mind with knowledge, challenge your assumptions, and stretch beyond your comfort zone daily. Growth happens at the edges of discomfort.

Your network is your net worth. Cultivate relationships with the care of a master gardener. Seek out mentors who challenge you to grow, partners who complement your strengths, and team members who share your vision. As you climb, never forget to reach back and lift others. True success is a rising tide that lifts all boats.

Strive for excellence in all you do, but remember - perfection is the enemy of progress. Focus instead on consistent, incremental improvement. Be 1% better today than you were yesterday. These small gains, compounded over time, lead to astonishing growth and legendary realities.

As you apply these principles, envision the ripple effect of your success. See the jobs you'll create, the problems you'll solve, and the lives you'll transform. Your success isn't just about you - it's about the positive change you'll catalyze in the world. Let this greater purpose fuel you when the journey gets tough.

Remember, legendary status isn't reserved for a select few. It's available to those who dare to dream big, work tirelessly, and persist in the face of adversity. You have already demonstrated immense courage by embarking on this entrepreneurial journey. Now, channel that same courage into becoming a legend in your field.

As you step forward into your extraordinary future, carry with you the wisdom of your past, the strength of your experiences, and the power of the principles we've explored. You are not just building a business; you are poised to become a transformative force within your industry and beyond. Let integrity be your foundation, innovation your toolset, and positive impact your ultimate measure of success.

As you close this book, know that you carry with you not just strategies and principles, but the collective wisdom and support of countless entrepreneurs who have walked this path before you. You are part of a legacy of dreamers and doers who have shaped the world we live in.

The pen is in your hands - what story will you write? What problems will you solve? What innovations will you bring to life? The world is waiting, full of possibilities, ripe for the impact only you can make.

Remember, your journey doesn't end here - it's just beginning. The principles we've discussed are your foundation, but your passion, your perseverance, and your unique vision are the true catalysts of your legendary realities.

Welcome to your extraordinary future. The world is waiting for you to make your mark. Now, go forth with confidence, determination, and the unshakable belief that your entrepreneurial journey has prepared you for greatness.

The future is yours to shape. Now, go make history!

BIBLIOGRAPHY

Bloomenthal, Andrew. "Oprah Winfrey: Early Life and Education, Notable Accomplishments, and Philanthropy." Investopedia. Updated January 10, 2024. Accessed July 31, 2024. https://www.investopedia.com/articles/insights/072816/how-did-oprah-winfrey-get-rich.asp.

Buchanan, Naomi. "Microsoft CEO Nadella Says He's 'Optimistic' About AI's Future and Global Standards." Investopedia. Published January 16, 2024. Accessed July 31, 2024. https://www.investopedia.com/microsoft-ceo-satya-nadella-says-he-is-optimistic-about-the-future-of-ai-and-global-standards-8426736.

Dweck, Carol S. Mindset: The New Psychology of Success. New York: Random House, 2006. 14.

Epictetus. "It's not what happens to you, but how you react to it that matters." Commonly attributed quote.

"Flex-N-Gate Overview." Zippia. Accessed July 1, 2024. https://www.zippia.com/flex-n-gate-careers-23580/.

Ford, Henry. "Whether you think you can, or you think you can't - you're right." Commonly attributed quote.

Goleman, Daniel. Emotional Intelligence: Why It Can Matter More Than IQ (1995; repr., London: Bloomsbury, 2009), 10.

Hopkins, Tom. "I am not judged by the number of times I fail, but by the number of times I succeed. And the number of times I succeed is in direct proportion to the number of times I can fail and keep on trying." Commonly attributed quote.

Julia Hanna, "Power Posing: Fake It Until You Make It," Business Research for Business Leaders, Harvard Business Reviews, September 20, 2010, https://hbswk.hbs.edu/item/power-posing-fake-it-until-you-make-it.

"Philip Emeagwali." Computer Scientists of the African Diaspora. Accessed August 25, 2024. https://www.math.buffalo.edu/mad/computer-science/emeagwali_philip.html.

Schultz, Howard. Pour Your Heart Into It: How Starbucks Built a Company One Cup at a Time (New York: Hyperion, 1997), 10.

The Holy Bible: New King James Version. Nashville: Thomas Nelson, 1982.

The Nobel Prize. "Wangari Maathai Facts." *The Nobel Peace Prize 2004*. Accessed August 25, 2024. https://www.nobelprize.org/prizes/peace/2004/maathai/facts/.

Tolstoy, Leo. "The two most powerful warriors are patience and time." Commonly attributed quote.

Twain, Mark. "The two most important days in your life are the day you are born and the day you find out why." Commonly attributed quote.

www.ingramcontent.com/pod-product-compliance
Lightning Source LLC
Chambersburg PA
CBHW070803100426
42742CB00012B/2234